THE CRABAPPLE BAKERY
cupcake
COOKBOOK

JENNIFER GRAHAM

PENGUIN BOOKS

PENGUIN BOOKS

THE CRABAPPLE BAKERY
cupcake
COOKBOOK

PENGUIN BOOKS

Published by the Penguin Group
Penguin Group (Australia)
250 Camberwell Road, Camberwell, Victoria 3124, Australia
(a division of Pearson Australia Group Pty Ltd)
Penguin Group (USA) Inc.
375 Hudson Street, New York, New York 10014, USA
Penguin Group (Canada)
90 Eglinton Avenue East, Suite 700, Toronto ON M4P 2Y3, Canada
(a division of Pearson Penguin Canada Inc.)
Penguin Books Ltd
80 Strand, London WC2R 0RL, England
Penguin Ireland
25 St Stephen's Green, Dublin 2, Ireland
(a division of Penguin Books Ltd)
Penguin Books India Pvt Ltd
11 Community Centre, Panchsheel Park, New Delhi – 110 017, India
Penguin Group (NZ)
67 Apollo Drive, Rosedale, North Shore 0632, New Zealand
(a division of Pearson New Zealand Ltd)
Penguin Books (South Africa) (Pty) Ltd
24 Sturdee Avenue, Rosebank, Johannesburg 2196, South Africa

Penguin Books Ltd, Registered Offices: 80 Strand, London, WC2R 0RL, England

First published by Penguin Group (Australia), 2007

16 15 14 13 12 11 10 9 8

Many thanks go to Danielle Toigo of Creative Homewares in Albert Park, Victoria,
who provided a selection of the beautiful props.

Fabric credits: Lightning Bugs and Other Mysteries by Heather Koss for Free Spirit, www.freespiritfabric.com,
pages 42, 78 & 119; Petite Fleur by P&B Textiles, www.pbtex.com, pages 107 & 131; Judie Rothermel (Aunt Grace
Scrapbag), Marcus Brothers Textiles Inc., www.marcusbrothers.com, pages 30, 36 & 137; Dottie by Moda Fabrics,
www.modafabrics.com, pages 54 & 108.

Every effort has been made to trace and acknowledge copyright material. The publisher
would be pleased to hear from any copyright holders who have not been acknowledged.

Cover and text design by Claire Tice © Penguin Group (Australia)
Photographs by Julie Renouf
Typeset in Avenir and DIN by Post Pre-Press Group, Brisbane, Queensland
Colour reproduction by Splitting Image, Clayton, Victoria
Printed in China by Everbest Printing Co. Ltd

National Library of Australia Cataloguing-in-Publication data:

Graham, Jennifer.
The Crabapple Bakery cupcake cookbook.
Includes index.
ISBN: 978 0 14300 494 3.
1. Cake. 2. Cake decorating. I. Title.

641.8653

penguin.com.au

contents

a word from Jennifer

As the founder and director of The Crabapple Cupcake Bakery and author of this very special cupcake book, I am delighted and proud to share with you many of the cupcake recipes that I produce at the bakery. The recipes have been adapted so that you can create small numbers of these cupcakes and layer cakes for your family and friends to wow over, and you can be proud to say 'I made them myself'.

My philosophy has always been that you should have fun when baking and decorating cakes. I believe in the real emotions that are baked and decorated into your beautiful cake or cupcakes, rather than any hard and fast rules. The best advice I can give you is to have patience. Don't be disappointed if your first attempt is not exactly like the photograph – remember, I have had years of practice. I am not industry trained and it took me more than a year to perfect the vanilla cupcake. So, if you are not entirely happy with your first effort, have a cup of tea (from a china cup of course!), enjoy tasting what you have made, and then try again.

Once you have made a few of the recipes in this book, why not have a go at creating your very own masterpiece? I would be absolutely delighted to receive photographs of your beautiful creations – I will place them on the The Friends of Crabapple page of my website, www.crabapplecupcakebakery.com.au, for others to wow over.

Kindest Regards

Jennifer Graham

the Crabapple Cupcake Bakery story

Jennifer Graham started out making cupcakes to display on the range of old-fashioned cake stands she was selling at craft markets around Victoria, in a bid to encourage customers to buy her wares. After only a couple of weeks the customers were not coming to buy her cake stands but to buy her beautiful cupcakes.

After only six weeks Jennifer found herself in the cupcake business and set out to make the most beautiful cupcakes in the world. The Crabapple Cupcake Bakery was born. For the next 18 months the business involved the entire family. Jennifer baked all the cupcakes in her home oven, decorating the larger cakes herself and designing ever-more intricate cupcakes. Her husband John quit his job and looked after the making of the tiered cupcake stands, packing all the cookies, boiling up the plum puddings and getting everything and everyone to market each week-end. Their three daughters Natalie, Hayley and Laura became creative cupcake decorators, with Hayley (only 14 at the time) designing the Crabapple signature swirl that the bakery is now known for.

Jennifer worked diligently to master the best vanilla cupcake recipe and then increase the range of cakes to 40 flavours, while the decorators kept coming up with more and more beautiful designs. It wasn't long before a shop was sought, to house the now vast array of baking equipment and ingredients. A shop in the village of Tecoma in Victoria was eventually chosen. The Crabapple Cupcake Bakery was to produce more and more cupcakes over the next three years, until they were making up to 5000 cupcakes a week in the busy season. A factory was the next logical step.

The Crabapple Cupcake Bakery became a company in May 2006 and moved to its present address in Ferntree Gully. The Ferntree Gully factory supplies cupcakes to independent supermarkets and cafés, and for corporate functions and weddings. The bakery has been featured in numerous shop displays, wedding and lifestyle magazines, television programs, newspaper articles, gift catalogues and books. The Crabapple Cupcake Bakery even created cupcakes for Robert Gordon Pottery, which were turned into beautiful ceramic trinket boxes.

The Crabapple Cupcake Bakery retail store is situated in the Prahran Market in Victoria, where cupcakes are baked fresh daily and are presented on pretty floral china, with pots of tea served up in original silver Robur teapots.

tips, techniques & tools

how to bake a great cake

Here are some very basic rules you can follow to help you bake consistently good cakes and cupcakes.

THE RECIPE

Read the entire recipe to make sure that you have all the ingredients and understand the method. By reading the recipe thoroughly before you start, you'll be less likely to prolong the mixing process, which can ruin your cake.

THE KEY INGREDIENTS

BUTTER The best butter for cakes is from New Zealand, as it has a higher butterfat content than Australian butter. It's also the best butter for cookie baking. Butter should always be used at room temperature, unless otherwise specified. If your butter is too cold, microwave it for 5 seconds at a time until it is soft but not runny.

WHITE SUGAR Not all sugar is good sugar. Some brands of white sugar do not dissolve properly when creamed with butter, and can remain like sand in the mix. I recommend CSR White Sugar.

EGGS Cakes just love eggs, and the larger the better. I only use 67–70 g eggs. If you only have small eggs (50 g), add an extra egg for every four eggs required. Like butter, eggs are best used at room temperature. In the wintertime I have been known to place the eggs in a basin of warm water until I am ready to use them. Follow the method carefully when adding eggs to your mixture in order to achieve the most consistent results.

VANILLA I use vanilla extract, as it tastes better than vanilla essence. If you use essence instead, you will need to add half as much again to the amount the recipe requires. I do not recommend using vanilla flavouring as it makes a very sweet, unpleasant-tasting cake.

MILK Always use full cream milk, as all cakes taste better with the higher fat content. Milk must be at room temperature when used, as cold milk will cause the mixture to shrink and the end result will be a tough cake. Microwave cold milk for about 1 minute to warm it up before use.

PLAIN FLOUR I recommend using cake flour, but it is not always readily available. Well-sifted plain flour is acceptable as long as it is fresh and a good quality brand.

SELF-RAISING FLOUR I prefer to make my own self-raising flour from plain flour mixed with either baking powder or bicarbonate of soda – each recipe has the ratio of flour to rising agent listed in the ingredients. Whether you use baking powder or bicarbonate of soda will depend on the acid content and rising requirements of the particular mixture (see Baking Powder and Bicarbonate of Soda below). If using shop-bought self-raising flour I purchase a quality brand.

BAKING POWDER Baking powder is similar to bicarbonate of soda, but has two extra acids that help with the aeration and rising of the cake mixture. Baking powder is used in recipes where there are no acidic ingredients, and its acidic properties cause two chemical reactions. The first reaction takes place when the baking powder comes in contact with the wet ingredients and creates carbon dioxide bubbles in the mixture, helping to aerate it. The second reaction takes place when the mixture comes in contact with heat during the baking process, causing it to rise. Baking powder must always be fresh – if it's more than 1 year old it will be almost useless.

BICARBONATE OF SODA Bicarbonate of soda (baking soda) is used in recipes where there are acidic ingredients – i.e. bananas, buttermilk, brown sugar, honey, fruit juice, sour cream, natural cocoa, etc. When the bicarbonate of soda comes into contact with the acidic ingredients as well as moisture, carbon dioxide is created. Cakes of this kind need to be baked as soon as possible after mixing, as the mixture will begin to rise immediately. Note: Bicarbonate of soda should never be used instead of baking powder in butter cakes or they will come out looking very brown, and tasting like soap.

DARK CHOCOLATE I recommend you only use high quality couverture chocolate, which contains at least 32 per cent cocoa butter (the higher the cocoa butter content, the better the chocolate). Compound chocolate has a lower cocoa butter content, and more sugar. I do not recommend using chocolate chips for melting as they have very low cocoa butter content and very high sugar. Chocolate chips should only be used when baking chocolate chip cupcakes. When melting chocolate, use a double boiler – be careful not to let any water get into the chocolate – or place the chocolate in a metal bowl over a large saucepan of simmering water, making sure the water does not touch the bowl. Chocolate will burn if you try to melt it over direct heat.

WHITE CHOCOLATE White chocolate is made primarily of milk, sugar and cocoa butter. It contains no cocoa solids at all. Good quality white chocolate is recommended, and should have a cocoa butter content of at least 20 per cent. When melting, use a double boiler (see Dark Chocolate, above). Note that white chocolate takes longer to melt than dark chocolate.

THE METHOD

Careful reading of the method is one of the most important components of baking a great cake. It gives you a clear understanding of the construction of a cake batter and the time that it will take to complete.

PREPARATION OF BAKING TINS Always prepare your baking tins before you begin, as the cake mixture will start to rise immediately and should go into the oven as soon as possible once it is complete. Line cake tins with baking paper, place cupcake papers into muffin trays, and grease dariole moulds with a canola-oil spray.

CREAMING When creaming the butter and sugar, always start with the butter and then add the sugar. If you put the sugar in first you will have trouble combining the mixture. First, cream the butter for 1–2 minutes using an electric mixer on medium speed – this will allow aeration to begin before you add the sugar. Then add the sugar in two or three batches, so that you don't choke the butter. Beat for about 2 minutes after each addition – this will keep the mixture light and the sugar will have a chance to start dissolving. Scrape the sides and bottom of the bowl after each addition to make sure the mixture is evenly beaten.

EGGS Eggs should be added one or two at a time and beaten for the stated time after each addition, or until the mixture is light and fluffy.

WET AND DRY INGREDIENTS The dry ingredients should be sifted together and added on the lowest speed of the electric mixer. Dry ingredients should be added alternately with the wet ingredients (such as yoghurt, milk, buttermilk), with dry ingredients added first and last. Make sure you scrape the sides and bottom of the bowl between additions. Do not beat any longer than required as this will toughen the mixture and you'll end up with heavy cupcakes.

ADDITIONS Additions such as chocolate chips, chopped nuts, and berries, should be folded in after the wet and dry ingredients.

DIVIDING THE MIXTURE I use an ice-cream scoop to spoon the mixture into cupcake papers. While each recipe in this book tells you how many cupcakes it will make, this number is approximate only – the size of the cupcake papers you use will determine how many cupcakes you'll be able to make.

BAKING Your oven needs to be set at the specified temperature before you start preparing your mixture, so that it has reached the exact temperature by the time you are ready to bake. I highly recommend that you buy an oven thermometer, which remains permanently in your oven and correctly measures the temperature (see Tools of the Trade, page 17). You then heat your oven according to the thermometer, not the oven dials – domestic ovens can heat up to 40°C higher than the dial reading!

Bake cakes for the specified time or until a fine skewer inserted into the centre of the cake comes out clean. Remove from the oven immediately and cool on a wire rack for the specified time before frosting.

STORAGE Frosted and unfrosted cupcakes should always be stored in an airtight container. Some cupcakes keep better than others, so always check the recipe and make sure you eat them while they're still fresh.

simple decorating techniques

When it comes to decorating cakes and cupcakes the first thing to remember is just have fun. Don't be afraid to use your imagination and be creative. I love to decorate my cakes and cupcakes with little bits and pieces I find at the shopping centre (such as the fairies on the Vanilla Fairy Birthday Cake). Not everything you put on cakes and cupcakes has to be edible – it just has to look good!

FROSTING A CUPCAKE

Before you can frost a cupcake you need to know what look you are trying to achieve. This will determine the type of frosting you choose, the style of application you'll use, and the tools you'll require.

Fluffy frostings such as buttercream, fudge frosting, ganache and cream cheese are probably the easiest for beginners to work with. It doesn't matter how new you are to decorating, you can achieve great results with these frostings the first time. The Crabapple signature swirl may take a little while to master, but persevere – by carefully following the steps in this section, you'll soon achieve your desired look.

CRABAPPLE SIGNATURE SWIRL

The frosting should be soft – the consistency of whipped cream.

1 Using a round-edged kitchen knife, put a dollop of frosting in the middle of the cupcake.
2 Use the knife to push the frosting towards the edge of the cupcake. Begin turning the cupcake anti-clockwise while at the same time pushing the frosting clockwise.
3 Then, working from the edge of the cupcake, push the frosting back towards the middle, until you create a central peak.
4 Decorate immediately.

FROSTINGS MOST SUITED TO THIS TECHNIQUE

- Chocolate Fudge Frosting
- Real Caramel Sauce Frosting
- White Chocolate Ganache
- Dark Chocolate Ganache
- Vanilla Buttercream

FLAT SPATULA

- Using an offset palette knife, put a dollop of frosting in the middle of the cupcake.
- Use the knife to spread the frosting in an even layer over the cupcake. Starting from one side, move the knife back and forth across the frosting, working towards the opposite side until you have a flat smooth surface.
- Decorate immediately.

FROSTINGS MOST SUITED TO THIS TECHNIQUE

- Chocolate Fudge Frosting
- Dark Chocolate Ganache
- Nutella Frosting
- Vanilla Buttercream
- Cream Cheese Frosting
- Marshmallow Frosting
- Real Caramel Sauce Frosting
- White Chocolate Ganache

SOFT-SERVE

Put the frosting into a piping bag with coupler and chosen tip attached.

1 Pipe frosting in a circular motion, starting around the edge of the cupcake, to form a soft-serve ice-cream effect.

2 Decorate immediately.

FROSTINGS MOST SUITED TO THIS TECHNIQUE

- Chocolate Fudge Frosting
- Dark Chocolate Ganache
- Nutella Frosting
- Vanilla Buttercream
- Cream Cheese Frosting
- Marshmallow Frosting
- Real Caramel Sauce Frosting
- White Chocolate Ganache

PIPED LEAVES

- Prepare buttercream so that it is the consistency of butter at room temperature – if it is too cold the leaves will be difficult to pipe, and if it's too warm the leaves won't hold their shape.
- Put the buttercream into a piping bag with coupler and leaf tip #66 attached. Hold the piping tip on a 45-degree angle and apply gentle pressure to the bag. As the icing starts to appear, lift the icing bag up and down slightly and you will see the leaf start to form. As you reach the desired length of the leaf, relieve the pressure on the bag until the leaf starts to form a point.
- Release pressure completely and pull the bag away to leave you with a finished leaf.

FROSTINGS MOST SUITED TO THIS TECHNIQUE

- Vanilla Buttercream

HAND MOULDED

- Use your hands to roll a large spoonful of icing into a ball about the size of a peach.
- Place the ball on top of the cupcake and use your hands and fingers to create the shape you desire.
- Decorate immediately.

FROSTINGS MOST SUITED TO THIS TECHNIQUE

- Coconut Ice only

DIPPED

Icing should be prepared to a dipping consistency – like custard.

- Dip the top of the cupcake into the icing and remove any excess with a knife or the edge of the bowl.
- Let the icing set partially before decorating.

FROSTINGS MOST SUITED TO THIS TECHNIQUE

- Dark Chocolate Ganache
- Simple Icing
- Quick Royal Icing
- White Chocolate Ganache

POURED

- Prepare icing to pouring consistency – like thick pouring cream.
- Place cake or cupcakes on a wire rack and pour frosting over. Let the frosting partially set before decorating.

NOTE Poured frosting is only suitable for use on cakes or small darioles without cupcake papers.

FROSTINGS MOST SUITED TO THIS TECHNIQUE

- Dark Chocolate Ganache
- Orange Juice Icing
- Simple Icing
- Quick Royal Icing
- Passionfruit Icing
- White Chocolate Ganache

FREE-FORM SWIRL

- Using a round-edged kitchen knife, place a big dollop of frosting onto the top of the cupcake and spread out to the edges.
- With the knife, swirl the excess frosting using a circular flicking motion to create a fluffy peaked free-form swirl.

- Chocolate Fudge Frosting
- Dark Chocolate Ganache
- Nutella Frosting
- Vanilla Buttercream
- Cream Cheese Frosting
- Marshmallow Frosting
- Real Caramel Sauce Frosting
- White Chocolate Ganache

MOUNDED

- Using a round-edged kitchen knife, place a dollop of frosting into the centre of the cupcake.
- Spread the frosting downwards to cover the edges, then smooth until you have a dome shape.

FROSTINGS MOST SUITED TO THIS TECHNIQUE

- Chocolate Fudge Frosting
- Dark Chocolate Ganache
- Nutella Frosting
- Vanilla Buttercream
- Cream Cheese Frosting
- Marshmallow Frosting
- Real Caramel Sauce Frosting
- White Chocolate Ganache

FONDANT

TO COLOUR

- Flatten out the fondant with your hands.
- Dip a toothpick into the required colour and use this to apply the required amount of food colouring to the fondant, then fold each edge of the icing in towards the centre.
- Knead and fold the icing like you would bread dough. Continue to stretch and fold the icing until you achieve an even colour.
- You can add extra colour at any time, just remember to fold the icing in over the colouring so you don't end up with colouring on your bench top.

TO ROLL OUT

- Roll the icing into a smooth ball and flatten out with your hands.
- Dust a work surface with icing sugar and use a rolling pin to roll out the icing to the desired thickness.
- You can now cut out whatever shape you desire.

FROSTING A LAYER CAKE

1 FILLING

To fill a layer cake, start with two cakes of the same size. Cut the top off each cake using a bread knife, to create a flat top. Place one of the cakes onto a cake board that is 3–5 cm larger than the size of the cake (e.g. a 20-cm cake would require a 23–25-cm cake board). Place a large amount of your chosen filling onto the top of the cake. Using an offset palette knife, smooth out the filling to the thickness you desire – keep the filling a couple of centimetres from the edge. Place the second cake upside down on top of the first. Press down gently.

2 CRUMB COATING

The crumb coating is like an undercoat – it provides a smooth canvas upon which to create your masterpiece. To apply the crumb coating, use an offset palette knife to spread a thin layer of your chosen frosting over the top and sides of the cake, making sure to fill the gap between the layers with extra frosting. Leave in the fridge for about 5 minutes to set.

3 FROSTING

Once the crumb coating has set, spread a thick layer of frosting over the top and sides of the cake. Then use the spatula to create some swirls in the frosting. Try to achieve a fluffy look.

4 DECORATING

One way to create a simple but beautiful decoration is to pipe round or star-shaped blobs around the top and bottom edges of the cake. Attach a round or star tip to a piping bag and pipe some balls of frosting close together around the bottom of the cake. Then pipe eight high swirls evenly around the edge of the top of the cake. Use some of the ideas suggested in this book to add extra decorations to your cake, or better still, use your imagination to create your own unique masterpiece.

NOTE Frostings and fillings should always be stored in the refrigerator – either in an airtight container or in a bowl tightly covered with plastic film. Lemon curd and sauces can be stored in a glass jar in the fridge.

tools of the trade

A cake decorator should no sooner consider starting work without the right equipment than a builder would consider constructing a house without the right tools. You don't need to spend lots of money to get started. With this book I have used just a few tools to create a number of different styles, so that you can enjoy making all of the cupcakes featured with little expense. I have included a couple of more decadent extras for the decorations, such as the glitter, but these are optional.

OVEN THERMOMETER Don't even think of baking seriously without an oven thermometer (see How to Bake a Great Cake, page 10). They are available from any homewares store.

ELECTRIC MIXER If you don't own a mixer, don't go out and buy the biggest and the best – a hand-held electric mixer will do. The first six months I was in business I managed quite well with a second-hand mixer.

BAKING TINS Cupcake and cake tins are readily available from the supermarket and homewares stores. Dariole moulds can be found at some homewares stores and cookware supply stores. Tins are available in aluminium, silicon, non-stick and other varieties. I don't have a preference for any particular kind.

CUPCAKE PAPERS A huge range of colours and designs are available from supermarkets, homewares stores and decorating suppliers.

UTENSILS Ice-cream scoops, palette knives, slotted metal spoons, wooden spoons, rubber spatulas, piping bags and tips, scone cutters, brushes and whisks are available from supermarkets and homewares stores. (Note that some shops may call an offset palette knife an offset spatula or a crank-handled spatula.)

MEASURING EQUIPMENT Measuring cups, measuring spoons, measuring jugs and scales are available from supermarkets and homewares stores.

INGREDIENTS Almost every ingredient I purchased for my first year in business was from the supermarket. You may need to visit a specialty food shop for some of the ingredients, such as Billington's sugar, fondant and good-quality chocolate.

DECORATIONS Food colouring, edible glitter and lustre dust, cachous, sprinkles, sugar flowers and stars, plastic figurines, candles, fondant and sprays are available from a variety of locations – supermarkets, homewares stores, decorating suppliers and gift shops. (See the suppliers list on page 165.)

In this book, 'sprinkles' refer to elongated sprinkles (and in one case, heart-shaped sprinkles), while 'nonpareils' refer to the spherical kind that you find in Hundreds and Thousands. Nonpareils sold as individual colours (not mixed) can be difficult to find, but are available from the Crabapple Bakery and other specialty stores.

When using fondant (sometimes called 'plastic icing'), I prefer Orchard Ready Made Icing, which is available from many supermarkets in a range of colours.

Note that the food colouring used in this book is always liquid, except when specified as Wilton's. Wilton's colouring is in paste form, and gives a stronger colour to your icing. Use a toothpick to add this colouring to your icing in tiny amounts, until you reach the desired shade.

cupcakes

vanilla daisy cupcakes

The vanilla cupcake is the epitome of what a cupcake represents, and is by far the biggest seller at the bakery. You can frost this cake with almost any flavour of icing. Here we've topped it with simple coloured buttercreams and sugar daisies.

2¾ cups plain flour

2 teaspoons baking powder

200 g softened unsalted butter

1¾ cups castor sugar

4 eggs

1 tablespoon vanilla extract

1 cup milk

Crabapple Bakery's vanilla cakes

MAKES 24 KEEPS 2 days FREEZES 2 months

Preheat oven to 170°C. Line two 12-hole muffin trays with cupcake papers.

Sift together the flour and baking powder. In a separate bowl, cream the butter for 1–2 minutes. Add the castor sugar a third at a time, beating for 2 minutes after each addition. After the last addition, beat until the mixture is light and fluffy and the sugar has almost dissolved. Add eggs one at a time, beating for 1 minute after each addition or until mixture is light and fluffy. Add the vanilla extract and beat until combined.

Add a third of the flour to the creamed mixture and beat on low speed until combined. Add half of the milk and beat until combined. Repeat this process. Add the remaining third of the flour and beat until thoroughly combined; do not over-beat as this will toughen the mixture.

Spoon mixture into cupcake papers, filling each about three-quarters full. Bake for 18–20 minutes or until a fine skewer inserted comes out clean. Remove cupcakes from the trays immediately and cool on a wire rack for 30 minutes before frosting.

continued

1 quantity Vanilla Buttercream
(page 142)

food colouring: pink, yellow,
blue, violet, apple-green,
peach

24 sugar daisies

multicoloured sprinkles

decoration

Divide buttercream evenly between six small cups. Add a drop of one food colouring to each of the cups and mix, to create six coloured frostings.

Using a round-edged kitchen knife, apply the buttercream in the Crabapple signature swirl (see page 12). Working quickly, before the buttercream dries, top each cupcake with a sugar daisy and some sprinkles.

dinosaur rock cupcakes

This is my favourite chocolate cupcake recipe. The staff at the bakery like to take these cakes from the rack and eat them while they're still warm.

3 cups plain flour

2 teaspoons bicarbonate
   of soda

1 teaspoon baking powder

1 teaspoon salt

3 tablespoons instant
   coffee granules

1 cup hot water

1 cup cocoa

1 cup cold water

200 g softened unsalted
   butter

2½ cups castor sugar

4 eggs

1 tablespoon vanilla extract

chocolate birthday cakes

MAKES 24 KEEPS 2 days FREEZES 2 months

Preheat oven to 170°C. Line two 12-hole muffin trays with chocolate-coloured cupcake papers.

Sift together the flour, bicarbonate of soda, baking powder and salt. In a separate bowl whisk together the coffee, hot water and cocoa until you have a smooth paste. Add the cold water and whisk until evenly combined.

In a separate bowl, cream the butter for 1–2 minutes. Add the castor sugar a third at a time, beating for 2 minutes after each addition. After the last addition, beat until the mixture is light and fluffy and the sugar has almost dissolved. Add eggs one at a time, beating for 1 minute after each addition or until mixture is light and fluffy. Add the vanilla extract and beat until combined.

Add a quarter of the flour to the creamed mixture and beat on low speed until combined. Add a third of the cocoa mixture and beat until combined. Repeat this process twice more. Add the remaining quarter of the flour and beat until thoroughly combined; do not over-beat as this will toughen the mixture.

continued

Spoon mixture into cupcake papers, filling each about three-quarters full. To prevent the cupcakes cracking on top, allow the mixture to sit in the cupcake papers for 20 minutes before baking. Bake for 18–20 minutes or until a fine skewer inserted comes out clean. Remove cupcakes from the trays immediately and cool on a wire rack for 30 minutes before frosting.

1 quantity Vanilla Buttercream (page 142)

food colouring: apple-green, Wilton's buttercup yellow

24 dinosaur/star candles

chocolate sprinkles

chocolate rocks

decoration

Divide the buttercream into two small bowls. Add a couple of drops of apple-green food colouring to one bowl and a couple of drops of yellow to the other. Mix to create even colours.

Frost half the cupcakes with the yellow buttercream, and half with the green. Using a round-edged kitchen knife, apply the frosting in the Crabapple signature swirl (see page 12). Working quickly, before the buttercream dries, top each cupcake with a candle, and decorate with sprinkles and chocolate rocks.

strawberry
butterfly cupcakes

At the bakery we make our butterfly cupcakes using the Vanilla Cakes recipe. I have included this traditional sponge butterfly recipe so that you can use whichever version you prefer.

½ cup plain flour

½ cup self-raising flour

¼ cup cornflour

¼ cup custard powder

6 eggs

1 cup castor sugar

sponge butterfly cakes

MAKES 24 KEEPS 1 day FREEZES 2 weeks

Preheat oven to 170°C. Line two 12-hole muffin trays with cupcake papers.

Combine the flours and custard powder by sifting together three times.

In a separate bowl, beat the eggs for 1–2 minutes using an electric mixer on medium speed. Turn speed to high and beat for a further 15 minutes. Add the castor sugar gradually, beating until sugar has dissolved. Beat for a further 10 minutes or until light and fluffy.

Using a slotted metal spoon, fold the flour mixture through the egg mixture until just combined.

Spoon mixture into cupcake papers, filling each about three-quarters full. Bake for 12 minutes or until a fine skewer inserted comes out clean. Remove cupcakes from the trays immediately and cool on a wire rack for 30 minutes before cutting.

continued

¼ cup strawberry preserve

piping bag

star tip #9

1 quantity Jam and Cream
   Filling (page 155)

12 fresh strawberries, halved

icing sugar

decoration

Holding a sharp paring knife on a 45-degree angle, cut out a cone-shaped piece from the top of each cupcake. Cut this cone in half down the middle, to make the butterfly wings.

Place a teaspoon of strawberry preserve into the hole you have made in each cupcake. Over this, pipe a large rosette of jam and cream filling. Arrange the butterfly wings on top and place a strawberry half between the pair of wings. Dust lightly with sifted icing sugar.

These cupcakes should be eaten within 4 hours once decorated.

Lady Tarryn's wedding cakes

These cupcakes are named after the bride that I first designed them for. They have been a very popular cupcake for weddings ever since. The cake tastes like a very rich buttercake, keeps very well, and has the perfect texture for baking into moulded shapes.

4 cups plain flour

1½ teaspoons baking powder

500 g butter, chopped

2 cups milk

4 cups castor sugar

300 g white chocolate, chopped

4 eggs, whisked

2 teaspoons vanilla extract

white chocolate mud cakes

MAKES 20 darioles or 24 cupcakes
KEEPS 4 days FREEZES 2 months

Preheat oven to 155°C. Lightly grease 20 dariole moulds.

Sift flour and baking powder together into a large bowl. Make a well in the centre. Set aside. Put butter, milk, castor sugar and white chocolate into a metal bowl and place over a large saucepan of simmering water. Stir continuously using a flat-bottomed wooden spoon until chocolate has melted and sugar has dissolved. Remove from the heat and cool to room temperature.

Use a rubber spatula to fold the eggs and vanilla extract into the cooled chocolate mixture. Pour this mixture into the well in the flour and fold together until well combined.

Divide the mixture evenly between the dariole moulds. Bake for 30 minutes or until a fine skewer inserted comes out clean. Place moulds on a wire rack to cool for 10 minutes before turning out. Allow to cool for a further 30 minutes before frosting.

continued

If using regular cupcake papers instead of dariole moulds, this recipe will make 24 cupcakes. Cooking time may decrease slightly. Bake until a fine skewer inserted comes out clean.

RASPBERRY WHITE CHOCOLATE MUD CAKES
Add ¾ cup fresh or frozen raspberries to the batter just before spooning into cupcake papers. Bake at 155°C for 30 minutes. This version is not suitable for baking in dariole moulds.

1 quantity White Chocolate Ganache, warm (page 152)

20 silver 70-mm cake rounds

1 cup Simple Icing (page 145) or Quick Royal Icing (page 144)

food colouring: pink

20 pink sugar daisies

decoration

Using a sharp knife, cut the top off each cupcake to create a flat surface. Turn cupcakes upside down onto a footed cooling rack for icing.

Pour ganache over the cupcakes until they are just covered. Leave to set for 15 minutes. Pour over remaining ganache until each cupcake is completely covered, then leave to set for 30 minutes.

Carefully lift each cupcake onto a cake round. (To avoid leaving finger marks, lift the cupcakes with a small offset palette knife underneath and a wooden skewer poked into the top.)

Prepare the Simple Icing to a slow running consistency, adding a couple of drops of pink colouring during preparation to produce the desired colour. Pour a level tablespoon of icing over the top of each cupcake. With a circular motion, use the back of the tablespoon to smooth the icing and get it running down the sides a little. Add a sugar daisy to the top of each cupcake immediately. Leave to set for at least 30 minutes.

Valentine's cupcakes

This is a very light chocolate mudcake – perfect for people who love the intense flavour of chocolate but find most mudcakes too rich.

3 tablespoons instant coffee granules (espresso strength)

¾ cup hot water

250 g butter

300 g dark cooking chocolate, chopped

4 eggs

⅓ cup vegetable oil

½ cup buttermilk

2 cups plain flour

¼ teaspoon salt

1½ teaspoons baking powder

½ teaspoon bicarbonate of soda

2½ cups castor sugar

½ cup cocoa

chocolate mud cakes

MAKES 28 KEEPS 4 days FREEZES 2 months

Preheat oven to 160°C. Line three 12-hole muffin trays with 28 red foil cupcake cases.

Dissolve coffee in hot water. Put the butter, chocolate and dissolved coffee into a metal bowl and place over a large saucepan of simmering water. Stir continuously with a flat-bottomed wooden spoon until chocolate has melted. Remove from the heat and cool to room temperature.

In a separate bowl, whisk together eggs, vegetable oil and buttermilk until combined. In another bowl sift together flour, salt, baking powder, bicarbonate of soda, castor sugar and cocoa and mix until well combined. Make a well in the centre. Pour in the egg mixture and mix with a rubber spatula until well combined. Add the cooled chocolate mixture and mix in carefully until thoroughly combined.

Spoon mixture into cupcake cases, filling each to just over half full (this mixture rises a lot). You may have enough mixture for more than 28 cupcakes. Bake for 25 minutes or until a fine skewer inserted comes out clean. Remove cupcakes from the trays immediately and cool on a wire rack for 30 minutes before frosting.

continued

This cake mixture can be made the day before baking. Cover the bowl with plastic film and store at room temperature.

If using regular cupcake papers instead of foils, this recipe will make 24 cupcakes. Cooking time may increase slightly. Bake until a fine skewer inserted comes out clean.

1 egg white

red sugar heart sprinkles

red glitter

2 cups Quick Royal Icing
     (page 144)

food colouring: Wilton's black

piping bag

round tip #2

decoration

Using a very small brush, paint each red sugar heart with egg white and sprinkle with red glitter.

Prepare icing to a dipping consistency. Dip the tops of the cupcakes into the icing and then leave to set.

Add enough black food colouring to the remaining icing to make it black. Pipe a continuous black line of icing in a zigzag pattern across the top of each cupcake. While the icing is still wet, arrange five red sugar hearts on top – the black icing will help them to stick.

orange lattice cupcakes

Flourless cakes are very popular among our gluten-intolerant customers.
(I am actually gluten-intolerant myself, but not very good at sticking to my diet!)
Not only are these flourless cupcakes healthy, they also taste really good.

3 whole oranges, washed

4 cups almond meal

3 teaspoons baking powder

120 g softened butter

1¾ cups castor sugar

7 eggs

orange flourless cakes

MAKES 24 KEEPS 4 days FREEZES 2 months

In a heavy-based saucepan, cover the oranges with water
and bring to the boil. Turn the heat down and simmer for
approximately 1 hour or until the oranges are very soft. Let
the oranges cool a little and then blend in a food processor
until smooth.

Preheat oven to 160°C. Line two 12-hole muffin trays with
cupcake papers.

Combine almond meal and baking powder in a small bowl.

In a separate bowl, cream the butter for 1–2 minutes. Add
the castor sugar a third at a time, beating for 2 minutes after
each addition. After the last addition, beat until the mixture is
light and fluffy and the sugar has almost dissolved. Add eggs
one at a time, beating for 1 minute after each addition or until
mixture is light and fluffy.

Add half of the almond meal mixture to the creamed mixture and beat on low speed until combined. Add the pureed
oranges and beat until combined. Add the remaining almond
meal mix and beat until combined.

continued

Spoon mixture into cupcake papers, filling each about three-quarters full. Bake for 30 minutes or until the cupcakes look dry and are slightly browned. Remove cupcakes from the trays and cool on a wire rack for 40 minutes before frosting.

1 quantity White Chocolate Ganache (page 152)

piping bag

star tip #5

24 pink sugar roses

48 green sugar leaves

pink cachous

decoration

Use an offset palette knife to apply the ganache in the flat spatula style (see page 12). Pipe the remaining ganache in a lattice pattern on top of each cupcake. Place a sugar rose in the centre of each cupcake with two sugar leaves either side. Sprinkle over the pink cachous.

ginger lovers' cupcakes

This cake recipe was adapted from an English version that promotes Billington unprocessed sugar products. It has a true natural ginger flavour and will be appreciated by all diehard ginger lovers.

4 cups self-raising flour

2 tablespoons ground ginger

½ teaspoon salt

400 g unsalted butter

1½ cups Billington's molasses
   or dark muscovado sugar

¾ cup treacle

1¼ cups milk

4 eggs, beaten

1½ tablespoons ginger
   in syrup, drained and
   finely chopped

ginger cakes

MAKES 24 KEEPS 2 days FREEZES 2 months

Preheat oven to 150°C. Line two 12-hole muffin tins with cupcake papers.

Sift together flour, ground ginger and salt. In a heavy-based saucepan, melt butter, sugar and treacle over a low heat. Stir continuously with a flat-bottomed wooden spoon until the sugar has dissolved. Do not boil. Take off heat and cool for 3 minutes.

Add milk and stir carefully until well combined. Add the eggs and stir until well combined. Add the chopped ginger and stir in well. Add the sifted flour mixture and stir in carefully until smooth; do not over-mix as this will toughen the mixture.

Spoon mixture into cupcake papers, filling each about three-quarters full. Bake for 20 minutes or until a fine skewer inserted comes out clean. Remove the cupcakes from the trays immediately and cool on a wire rack for 30 minutes before frosting.

continued

1 quantity Cream Cheese
   Frosting (page 149)

1 tablespoon Buderim
   shredded ginger, finely
   chopped

12 ginger jelly bears

ground ginger, to sprinkle

decoration

Mix the shredded ginger into the frosting. Using a round-edged kitchen knife, apply the frosting to the cupcakes in the free-form swirl design (see page 14). Top each cupcake with a ginger bear and sprinkle with ground ginger.

John's Baci birthday cupcakes

My husband John received these cupcakes for his last birthday. If you love a dense fudgy chocolate cupcake as much as he does, then this will suit you to a tee. This cupcake is suitable for the gluten intolerant, and is also a favourite with brides and grooms – it makes the perfect chocolate cupcake wedding cake.

350 g butter

450 g dark cooking
  chocolate, chopped

2½ cups castor sugar

1½ cups almond meal

2 cups cocoa

10 eggs

2 teaspoons vanilla extract

chocolate flourless cakes

MAKES 26 KEEPS 1 week FREEZES 2 months

Preheat oven to 140°C. Line three 12-hole muffin trays with 26 blue foil cupcake cases.

Combine butter, chocolate and castor sugar in a heavy-based saucepan over low heat. Mix continuously with a flat-bottomed wooden spoon until melted and smooth. Sift the almond meal and cocoa into a bowl. Add the chocolate mixture and beat for 1 minute on low speed. The mixture should be thoroughly combined.

Add eggs two at a time, beating after each addition until the mixture is well combined; do not over-beat or too much air will be incorporated and the cupcakes will crack during baking. Add the vanilla extract and beat until combined.

continued

Divide mixture evenly between cupcake cases. Bake for 30 minutes or until a fine skewer inserted comes out clean. Remove cupcakes from the trays and cool on a wire rack for 40 minutes before frosting.

TO MAKE REGULAR CUPCAKES
If using regular cupcake papers instead of foils, this recipe will make 24 cupcakes. Cooking time may increase slightly. Bake until a fine skewer inserted comes out clean.

1 quantity Vanilla Buttercream (page 142)

26 Baci chocolates

silver cachous, assorted sizes

12 blue candles

13 silver candles

1 blue metallic spray

decoration

Using a round-edged kitchen knife, apply the buttercream in the Crabapple signature swirl (see page 12). Working quickly, before the buttercream dries, decorate each cupcake with a Baci chocolate and sprinkle with the assorted silver cachous. Place a candle behind the chocolate on each of the cupcakes. Insert the blue metallic spray into the remaining cupcake.

church picnic carrot cupcakes

These Carrot Cakes with Cream Cheese Frosting are healthy and delicious. They're a great option if you're looking for a cupcake that is not too sweet.

carrot cakes

MAKES 24 KEEPS 2 days FREEZES 2 months

4 cups self-raising flour

2 teaspoons bicarbonate of soda

1 tablespoon ground cinnamon

2 cups vegetable oil

2⅔ cups soft brown sugar

6 eggs

5 cups peeled grated carrot, firmly packed

2 cups chopped walnuts

1 cup sultanas

zest of 2 oranges

zest of 2 lemons

Preheat oven to 180°C. Line a 12-hole muffin tray with cupcake papers.

Sift together the self-raising flour, bicarbonate of soda and cinnamon. In a separate bowl, beat the vegetable oil, brown sugar and eggs using an electric mixer on medium speed. Beat for about 5 minutes or until thick and creamy.

Add the grated carrot, chopped walnuts, sultanas, and orange and lemon zest. Beat on low speed until combined.

Add the flour mixture and beat until thoroughly combined; do not over-beat as this will toughen the mixture.

Spoon mixture into cupcake papers, filling each about three-quarters full. Bake for 20 minutes or until a fine skewer inserted comes out clean. Remove the cupcakes from the trays immediately and cool on a wire rack for 30 minutes before frosting.

continued

¼ cup roasted walnuts

1 tablespoon soft
   brown sugar

1 teaspoon ground cinnamon

1 quantity Cream Cheese
   Frosting (page 149)

24 yellow country-style
   sugar daisies

decoration

In a mortar and pestle, crush the roasted walnuts into fine crumbs. (Alternatively, you can place the walnuts into a plastic bag and crush them with a rolling pin.) Add the crushed walnuts to a bowl with the sifted sugar and cinnamon and mix thoroughly.

Using a round-edged kitchen knife, apply the cream cheese frosting in a free-form swirl design (see page 14). Top each cupcake with a country-style daisy and sprinkle with the crushed walnut mix.

Natalie's banana fudge cupcakes

This cake recipe was inspired by my childhood growing up in Gympie, Queensland. With an abundance of bananas, everyone had a secret recipe for banana cake. This is my recipe, best made with over-ripe bananas. I have dedicated this cupcake to my eldest daughter Natalie, who indulges often.

3⅓ cups plain flour

2 teaspoons bicarbonate of soda

½ teaspoon salt

1 teaspoon ground cinnamon

⅛ teaspoon allspice

250 g softened unsalted butter

3 cups castor sugar

4 eggs

1 teaspoon vanilla extract

1 cup buttermilk

2 cups mashed over-ripe banana

¾ cup macadamias, chopped

banana and macadamia cakes

MAKES 24 KEEPS 2 days FREEZES 2 months

Preheat oven to 170°C. Line two 12-hole muffin trays with cupcake papers.

Sift together the flour, bicarbonate of soda, salt, cinnamon and allspice.

In a separate bowl, cream the butter for 1–2 minutes. Add the castor sugar a third at a time, beating for 2 minutes after each addition. After the last addition, beat until the mixture is light and fluffy and the sugar has almost dissolved.

Add eggs one at a time, beating for 1 minute after each addition or until mixture is light and fluffy. Add the vanilla extract and beat until combined.

continued

Add a third of the flour mixture to the creamed mixture and beat on low speed until combined. Add half of the buttermilk and half of the mashed banana and beat until combined. Repeat this process. Add the remaining third of the flour mixture and beat until thoroughly combined; do not over-beat as this will toughen the mixture. Add the chopped macadamias and beat until evenly combined.

Spoon mixture into cupcake papers, filling each about three-quarters full. Bake for 20 minutes or until a fine skewer inserted comes out clean. Remove the cupcakes from the trays immediately and cool on a wire rack for 30 minutes before frosting.

1 quantity Chocolate Fudge Frosting (page 143)

48 chocolate-coated macadamia nuts

48 whole unsalted macadamias

¼ cup white chocolate pieces, melted

decoration

Using a round-edged kitchen knife, apply the frosting in the Crabapple signature swirl (see page 12).

Decorate each cupcake with two chocolate-coated macadamias and two plain macadamias.

Use a teaspoon to drizzle some of the melted chocolate over each cupcake.

lumberjack cupcakes
with vanilla custard

This cupcake is a favourite for all who love date and apple. Serve with vanilla custard and/or ice-cream for a great dessert. Also delicious frosted with Cream Cheese frosting.

600 g Granny Smith apples, peeled, cored and finely chopped

300 g dates, pitted and diced

1½ teaspoons bicarbonate of soda

1½ cups boiling water

2½ cups plain flour

1 teaspoon ground cinnamon

½ teaspoon ground ginger

200 g softened butter

1½ cups castor sugar

2 eggs

1½ teaspoons vanilla extract

lumberjack cakes

MAKES 24 regular cupcakes or 18 super cupcakes
KEEPS 4 days FREEZES 2 months

Combine apple, dates, bicarbonate of soda and boiling water in a bowl. Cover with plastic film and leave overnight at room temperature to allow the apples and dates to soften and absorb some of the water.

Preheat oven to 180°C. Line two 12-hole muffin trays with cupcake papers.

Sift together the flour, cinnamon and ginger. In a separate bowl, cream the butter for 1–2 minutes. Add half of the castor sugar and beat for 2 minutes. Add the remaining castor sugar and beat for 2 minutes or until mixture is light and fluffy and the sugar has almost dissolved. Add eggs one at a time, beating for 1 minute after each addition or until mixture is light and fluffy. Add the vanilla extract and beat until combined.

Stir in the apple and date mixture using a rubber spatula. Add the sifted flour mixture and fold in until well combined.

continued

Spoon mixture into cupcake papers, filling each about three-quarters full. Bake for 20 minutes or until a fine skewer inserted comes out clean. Remove cupcakes from the trays immediately and cool on a wire rack for 30 minutes before frosting.

TO MAKE LARGE CUPCAKES
If you want a really hearty dessert, use 18 super cupcake papers instead of 24 regular-sized cupcake papers. Cooking time may increase slightly. Bake until a fine skewer inserted comes out clean.

1 litre vanilla custard

1 litre vanilla ice-cream

decoration

Carefully peel the wrappers away from the lumberjack cupcakes. Place upside down onto a serving plate. Heat the vanilla custard and pour over the cupcakes. Serve with a scoop of vanilla ice-cream.

tropical island cupcakes

This delectable moist cupcake is a great way to use up over-ripe bananas and pineapples. It's a very simple cake recipe – all the ingredients are mixed together in one bowl.

2 cups plain flour

1 cup self-raising flour

1 teaspoon bicarbonate of soda

1 teaspoon ground cinnamon

1 teaspoon ground ginger

2 × 450-g tins crushed pineapple, drained (reserve juice)

2 cups soft brown sugar

1 cup desiccated coconut

2 cups mashed over-ripe banana

4 eggs, whisked

1½ cups vegetable oil

½ cup reserved pineapple juice

hummingbird cakes

MAKES 20 KEEPS 2 days FREEZES 2 months

Preheat oven to 170°C. Line two 12-hole muffin trays with 10 pink and 10 golden-yellow cupcake papers.

In a very large bowl sift together flours, bicarbonate of soda, cinnamon and ginger. Add the remaining ingredients and mix together using a large rubber spatula. Stir until evenly combined.

Spoon mixture into cupcake papers, filling each about three-quarters full. Bake for 25 minutes or until a fine skewer inserted comes out clean. Remove cupcakes from the trays immediately and cool on a wire rack for 40 minutes before frosting.

continued

1 quantity Cream Cheese
Frosting (page 149)

2 cups shredded coconut

20 cocktail umbrellas

decoration

Using a round-edged kitchen knife, mound the frosting onto the cupcakes and smooth to create a dome (see page 15). Take a handful of shredded coconut and pat onto the cupcake until entirely covered. Top with an opened cocktail umbrella.

Brittany's fuss free muffin cupcakes

I wanted to include this muffin-style cupcake for those who are not big cake eaters. We have made these cupcakes many times for weddings and 21st birthday parties – they are a fuss-free way to create an impressive display of moist and tasty cupcakes.

250 g unsalted butter

2 cups natural yoghurt

4 eggs

2⅔ cups plain flour

1½ tablespoons baking powder

2 cups almond meal

1⅔ cups castor sugar

500 g frozen raspberries

½ cup flaked almonds

raspberry, almond and yoghurt cakes

MAKES 24 KEEPS 2 days FREEZES 2 months

Preheat oven to 180°C. Line two 12-hole muffin trays with cupcake papers.

Melt the butter in a small saucepan over low heat. Leave to cool a little, then pour into a bowl with the yoghurt and eggs and whisk until thoroughly combined.

In a separate bowl, sift together flour, baking powder and almond meal. Add the castor sugar and combine. Make a well in the centre and pour in the yoghurt mixture. Fold in gently using a rubber spatula; do not over-stir, the mixture should be quite lumpy. Add the raspberries and fold in to just incorporate.

Spoon mixture into cupcake papers, filling each about three-quarters full. Sprinkle the flaked almonds evenly over the top of the cupcakes. Bake for 25 minutes or until the cupcakes spring back when pressed. They should be slightly browned.

continued

Remove cupcakes from the trays immediately and cool on a wire rack for 30 minutes before frosting.

1 cup icing sugar

food colouring: brown and yellow

Letter B stamp (available from art supply stores)

24 white sugar medallions

piping bag

star tip #9

1 cup Vanilla Buttercream (page 142)

gold glitter

decoration

Sift icing sugar over the cooled cupcakes.

Add one drop of brown food colouring to ten drops of yellow food colouring to make a gold colour. Place an unused absorbent kitchen cloth onto a piece of greaseproof paper, and pour the gold colouring onto it, letting it absorb evenly. You can now use the cloth as a stamp pad. Stamp a gold letter B onto each of the sugar medallions. (You may need two quantities of the gold food colouring.)

Pipe a small swirl of buttercream in the centre of each cupcake. Place a medallion on top of each swirl and sprinkle with gold glitter.

market morning cupcakes

There is something very satisfying about an orange and poppy seed cake. When I go to the racecourse markets in Victoria to sell cupcakes, I have to arrive very early to start the 1½ hour set-up. Afterwards, I look forward to nothing more than a hot cup of Earl Grey tea and this Orange and Poppy Seed Cake with Orange Juice Icing.

⅔ cup poppy seeds

1¼ cups milk

3¾ cups plain flour

2½ teaspoons baking powder

¼ teaspoon salt

300 g softened unsalted
butter

zest of 2 oranges

2½ cups white sugar

5 eggs

1½ teaspoons vanilla extract

orange and poppy seed cakes

MAKES 24 loaf cakes or 30 regular cupcakes
KEEPS 2 days FREEZES 2 months

Soak the poppy seeds in the milk for at least half an hour.

Preheat oven to 170°C. Lightly grease three 8-hole mini-loaf tins.

Sift together flour, baking powder and salt.

In another bowl, cream the butter for 1–2 minutes. Add the orange zest and beat for 1 minute. Add the sugar a third at a time, beating for 2 minutes after each addition. After the last addition, beat until the mixture is light and fluffy and the sugar has almost dissolved.

Add eggs one at a time, beating for 1 minute after each addition or until the mixture is light and fluffy. Add the vanilla extract and beat until combined.

continued

Add a third of the flour mixture to the creamed mixture and beat on low speed until combined. Add half of the milk and poppy seed mixture and beat until combined. Repeat this process. Add the remaining third of the flour mixture and beat until thoroughly combined; do not over-beat as this will toughen the mixture.

Spoon mixture into mini-loaf tins, filling each about three-quarters full. Bake for 18 minutes or until a fine skewer inserted comes out clean. Remove from the oven and allow to cool for 5–10 minutes in the trays before turning out. Cool on a wire rack for a further 30 minutes before frosting.

TO MAKE REGULAR CUPCAKES

If using regular cupcake papers instead of mini-loaf tins, this recipe will make 30 cupcakes. Cooking time may decrease slightly. Bake until a fine skewer inserted comes out clean.

1 quantity Orange Juice Icing (page 148)

¼ cup poppy seeds

24 apricot sugar daisies

decoration

Use a small offset palette knife to apply the icing in the flat spatula style (see page 12). While the frosting is still wet, use a teaspoon to sprinkle poppy seeds around the edge of the top of each cupcake. Place a sugar daisy on top.

oh Christmas tree,
oh Christmas tree cupcakes

I couldn't count the number of Christmas tree cupcakes we make at the bakery each year. We make them in three sizes using green cupcake papers. The green foil cases featured here look even better, but they only come in one size. This is a great recipe for using up any leftover fruit mince that you may have.

1 cup shop-bought fruit mince

½ cup brandy

1 cup milk

3 cups plain flour

2 teaspoons baking powder

½ teaspoon ground cinnamon

½ teaspoon ground nutmeg

½ teaspoon ground cloves

200 g softened butter

2 cups soft brown sugar

4 eggs

1 tablespoon vanilla extract

fruit mince cakes

MAKES 24 KEEPS 2 days FREEZES 2 months

Preheat oven to 170°C. Line two 12-hole muffin trays with green foil cupcake cases.

Put the fruit mince and brandy in a bowl and mix until thoroughly combined. Add the milk and mix until combined.

In a separate bowl, sift together the flour, baking powder, and ground cinnamon, nutmeg and cloves.

In another bowl, cream the butter for 1–2 minutes. Add half the sugar and beat for 3 minutes. Add the remaining sugar and beat for a further 3 minutes, until the mixture is light and fluffy and the sugar has almost dissolved. Add eggs one at a time, beating for 1 minute after each addition or until mixture is light and fluffy. Add the vanilla and beat until combined.

continued

Add a third of the flour mixture to the creamed mixture and beat on low speed until combined. Add half of the fruit mince mixture and beat until combined. Repeat this process. Add the remaining third of the flour mixture and beat until thoroughly combined; do not over-beat as this will toughen the mixture.

Spoon mixture into cupcake cases, filling each about three-quarters full. Bake for 18–20 minutes or until a fine skewer inserted comes out clean. Remove cupcakes from the trays immediately and cool on a wire rack for 30 minutes before frosting.

24 bright yellow sugar stars

1 egg white

gold glitter

1 quantity Vanilla Buttercream (page 142)

food colouring: green

piping bag

star tip #9

gold, silver and green cachous, of assorted sizes

decoration

Using a small brush, paint each of the sugar stars with egg white. Sprinkle on the gold glitter.

Add ¼ teaspoon green food colouring to the buttercream and mix until you have an even colour. Pipe the frosting in a circular motion, starting around the edge of the cupcake, to form a soft-serve ice-cream effect. Place a sugar star in the centre of each cupcake and sprinkle cachous over to resemble coloured lights.

VARIATION
If you're not a big fan of fruit mince, you can use this decoration on the Crabapple Bakery's Vanilla Cakes (page 25) instead.

coconut
marshmallow clouds

This is a very light cupcake that I created to satisfy my need to have coconut cake in my life.

¾ cup shredded coconut

2⅓ cups plain flour

¼ teaspoon salt

2 teaspoons baking powder

3 eggs

3 egg whites, extra

200 g softened unsalted butter

1¾ cups castor sugar

1 tablespoon vanilla extract

1 cup coconut milk

coconut cakes

MAKES 24 KEEPS 3 days FREEZES 2 months

Preheat oven to 170°C. Line two 12-hole muffin tins with cupcake papers.

Using an electric food processor, process the coconut until very fine about 3 or 4 minutes. Add coconut to a bowl with sifted flour, salt and baking powder. Mix until evenly combined.

In a separate bowl combine eggs and egg whites. Do *not* beat.

In another bowl, cream the butter for 1–2 minutes. Add the castor sugar a third at a time, beating for 2 minutes after each addition. After the last addition, beat until the mixture is light and fluffy and the sugar has almost dissolved.

Add the eggs a quarter at a time, beating for 1 minute after each addition or until the mixture is light and fluffy. Add the vanilla extract and beat until combined.

continued

Add a third of the flour mixture and beat on low speed until combined. Add half of the coconut milk and beat until combined. Repeat this process. Add the remaining third of the flour mixture and beat until thoroughly combined; do not over-beat as this will toughen the mixture.

Spoon mixture into cupcake papers, filling each about three-quarters full. Bake for 18 minutes or until a fine skewer inserted comes out clean. Remove cupcakes from the trays immediately and cool on a wire rack for 30 minutes before frosting.

1 quantity Marshmallow Frosting (page 150)

large piping bag

star tip #11

24 pink sugar country daisies

decoration

Pipe the frosting in a circular motion, starting around the edge of the cupcake, to form a soft-serve ice-cream effect. Top each cupcake with a country daisy.

who's my favourite teddy bear? cupcakes

Partnered with my Real Caramel Sauce Frosting, these Brownie Fudge Cakes are perfect for that special someone in your life.

2 cups walnuts

225 g unsalted butter

500 g dark cooking chocolate, chopped

1½ cups soft brown sugar, firmly packed

1 cup white sugar

6 eggs, whisked

3 teaspoons vanilla extract

1½ cups plain flour

¾ teaspoon salt

1 cup dark chocolate chips

brownie fudge cakes

MAKES 24 KEEPS 1 week FREEZES 2 months

Preheat oven to 170°C. Line two 12-hole muffin trays with chocolate-coloured cupcake papers.

Spread the walnuts over a flat biscuit tray and bake in the oven for 20 minutes. Allow to cool and then chop.

Put butter and chocolate into a metal bowl and place over a large saucepan of simmering water. Stir continuously with a flat-bottomed wooden spoon until the butter and chocolate have melted and are well combined. Remove from heat and cool to room temperature.

Add brown sugar and white sugar to cooled chocolate mixture. Stir until well combined. Add the eggs and vanilla extract. Stir until well combined. Add the sifted flour, salt, chopped walnuts and chocolate chips. Stir until well combined.

continued

Divide the mixture evenly between the cupcake papers. Bake for 30 minutes. The top of the cupcakes should look dull – if they look shiny, bake for a further 5 minutes or until they start looking a bit dull. Remove cupcakes from the trays immediately and cool on a wire rack for 45 minutes before frosting.

1 quantity Real Caramel Sauce Frosting (page 147)

24 teddy bear chocolates

chocolate sprinkles

decoration

Using a round-edged kitchen knife, apply the frosting in the Crabapple signature swirl (see page 12). Place a teddy bear in the centre of each cupcake and top with chocolate sprinkles.

Christmastime cupcakes

This cupcake has the most amazing flavour. It is like hot spiced mocha in a cupcake paper. Sweetened with just a thin layer of Quick Royal Icing this cake is a real treat at Christmastime. Personally, I like to indulge myself all year round.

3 cups plain flour

2 teaspoons baking powder

1 teaspoon bicarbonate of soda

2 teaspoons mixed spice

pinch of salt

150 g dark chocolate, chopped

¼ cup instant coffee granules

1 cup boiling water

200 g softened unsalted butter

1½ cups dark brown sugar

4 eggs

1 teaspoon vanilla extract

½ cup sour cream

mocha spice cakes

MAKES 26 KEEPS 2 days FREEZES 2 months

Preheat oven to 200°C. Line three 12-hole muffin trays with 26 red foil cupcake cases.

Sift together the flour, baking powder, bicarbonate of soda, mixed spice and salt. In a heavy-based saucepan, combine the chocolate, coffee and boiling water over low heat. Stir continuously with a flat-bottomed wooden spoon until chocolate has melted. Do not boil.

In a separate bowl, cream the butter for 1–2 minutes. Add half of the sugar and beat for 2 minutes. Add the remaining sugar and beat for a further 2 minutes or until the mixture is light and fluffy and the sugar has mostly dissolved. Add eggs one at a time, beating for 1 minute after each addition or until mixture is light and fluffy. Add the vanilla and beat until combined.

Add a third of the flour mixture to the creamed mixture and beat on low speed until combined. Add half of the sour cream and beat until combined. Repeat this process. Add the remaining third of the flour mixture and beat until thoroughly combined; do not over-beat as this will toughen the mixture.

continued

Use a rubber spatula to fold in the mocha mixture a third at a time. Be gentle and do not over-stir. The mixture will be very thin.

Spoon mixture into cupcake papers, filling each about two-thirds full (this mixture rises quite a lot). Bake for 15–18 minutes. The cupcakes should look a little moist on top. Leave cupcakes to cool in the trays for 5 minutes only. They will shrink considerably. Remove cupcakes from the trays and cool on a wire rack for a further 30 minutes before frosting.

TO MAKE REGULAR CUPCAKES

If using regular cupcake papers instead of foils, this recipe will make 24 cupcakes. Oven temperature and cooking time remain the same.

decoration

2 quantities Quick Royal Icing (page 144)

green fondant

icing sugar, for dusting

small holly leaf cutter

red fondant (or a bag of Jaffas)

Prepare the Quick Royal Icing to dipping consistency. Dip each of the cupcakes into the icing to coat the top. Leave to set a little.

Dust a work surface with icing sugar and use a rolling pin to roll out the green fondant into a flat piece about 2 mm thick. Use the leaf cutter to cut out 52 holly leaves. Roll the red fondant into 45–50 small balls, about 1-cm wide. Decorate each cupcake with two holly leaves and one, two or three red berries.

caramel bliss cupcakes

When is a cupcake not a cupcake? When it's a Caramel Bliss Cupcake – a cupcake with no cake in it! I wanted to share this very simple recipe with you as it uses elements of other recipes in this book, is about the same size as a cupcake, is fabulous at a tea party or as a wedding cake, and tastes like absolute bliss.

24 butternut snaps

1 quantity Not-so-secret Caramel Filling (page 159)

butternut snap bases

MAKES 24 KEEPS 4 days

Preheat oven to 170°C.

Place a butternut snap biscuit over each hole of two 12-hole muffin trays. Bake for 5–8 minutes or until the biscuits are soft.

Remove from the oven and immediately push each soft biscuit down into the hole to form a 'cup'.

Using a teaspoon, evenly divide the caramel between the 24 'cups'.

continued

2 piping bags

star tip #7

1 quantity Marshmallow
Frosting (page 150)

¼ cup dark chocolate
pieces, melted

round tip #2

decoration

Fill a piping bag with star tip attached with the marshmallow frosting. Pipe the frosting in a circular motion, starting around the edge of the cupcake, to form a soft-serve ice-cream effect.

Fill the second piping bag, with round tip attached, with the melted chocolate and decorate each cupcake in a zigzag pattern.

eat dessert first cupcakes

Sticky date pudding with caramel sauce would have to be my all-time favourite dessert, so I just had to turn it into a cupcake.

450 g dates, pitted and diced

2¼ cups water

1 tablespoon fresh
   grated ginger

2 teaspoons bicarbonate
   of soda

2½ cups self-raising flour

¼ teaspoon ground cloves

¾ teaspoon mixed spice

120 g softened butter

1⅓ cups castor sugar

4 eggs

sticky date cakes

MAKES 26 KEEPS 4 days FREEZES 2 months

Put the dates and water into a heavy-based saucepan. Bring to the boil over a medium to high heat, stirring continuously with a flat-bottomed wooden spoon. Remove from heat and add ginger and bicarbonate of soda. Stir until well combined. Cover saucepan with plastic film and let mixture cool to room temperature. (This mixture is best made the day before to allow the dates to absorb more of the water.)

Preheat oven to 180°C. Line three 12-hole muffin trays with 26 gold foil cupcake cases.

Sift together self-raising flour, ground cloves and mixed spice.

In a separate bowl, cream the butter for 1–2 minutes. Add half the castor sugar and beat for 2 minutes. Add remaining castor sugar and beat for 2 minutes or until the mixture is light and fluffy and the sugar has almost dissolved.

Add eggs one at a time, beating for 1 minute after each addition or until mixture is light and fluffy. Use a rubber spatula to fold in the flour mixture until well combined. Fold in the cooled date mixture until thoroughly combined.

continued

Spoon mixture into cupcake papers, filling each about three-quarters full. Bake for 20 minutes or until a fine skewer inserted comes out clean. Remove cupcakes from the trays immediately and cool on a wire rack for 30 minutes before frosting.

TO MAKE REGULAR CUPCAKES
If using regular cupcake papers instead of foils, this recipe will make 24 cupcakes. Oven temperature and cooking time remain the same.

1 quantity Real Caramel Sauce Frosting (page 147)

1 quantity Gold-lustre White Chocolate Lattices (page 163)

gold cachous

gold glitter

decoration

Using a round-edged kitchen knife, apply the frosting in the Crabapple signature swirl (see page 12). Place a chocolate lattice on a 45-degree angle on the top of each cupcake and sprinkle with cachous and glitter.

Nana's 50th birthday cupcakes

These elegant cupcakes are ideal for those with discerning tastes.

1¾ cups self-raising flour

3¼ cups blanched
    almond meal

200 g softened butter

2 teaspoons finely grated
    orange zest

1⅔ cups castor sugar

2 eggs

¾ cup freshly squeezed
    orange juice

orange and almond cakes

MAKES 18 darioles FREEZES 2 months

Preheat oven to 155°C. Lightly grease 18 dariole moulds.

Sift together flour and almond meal.

In a separate bowl, cream the butter for 1–2 minutes. Add the orange zest and beat for 1 minute.

Add the castor sugar a third at a time, beating for 2 minutes after each addition. After the last addition, beat until the mixture is light and fluffy and the sugar has almost dissolved. Add eggs one at a time, beating for 1 minute after each addition or until mixture is light and fluffy.

Using a rubber spatula, fold through a third of the flour mixture until just combined. Fold in half of the orange juice. Repeat this process. Add the remaining third of the flour and fold through until thoroughly combined; do not over-mix as this will toughen the mixture.

continued

Spoon mixture into dariole moulds, filling each to just over half full (this mixture rises a lot). Bake for 20 minutes or until a fine skewer inserted comes out clean. Place moulds on a wire rack to cool for 10 minutes before turning out. Allow cupcakes to cool for a further 30 minutes before frosting.

These cakes are best kept frozen as they are delicate and crumble easily.

18 gold foil cupcake cases

1 quantity Orange Juice Icing (page 148)

18 apricot sugar dianthus flowers

gold cachous

decoration

Using a sharp knife, cut the top off each cake to create a flat surface. Turn upside down into the gold foils. Pour a level tablespoon of icing over the top of each cupcake. With a circular motion, use the back of the tablespoon to smooth the icing and get it running down the sides a little. Top each cupcake with a sugar dianthus and a few gold cachous.

Pauli's purple rose cupcakes

This is one of the best fruitcake cupcakes that I have ever tasted. It is a great option for weddings, as you get to have a traditional fruitcake, but at the same time have a funky cupcake wedding cake.

1 kg mixed dried fruit with cherries (preferably Australian)

½ cup slivered almonds

¼ cup brandy

2 cups plain flour

2 teaspoons mixed spice

½ teaspoon ground nutmeg

½ teaspoon ground cinnamon

¼ teaspoon ground ginger

¼ teaspoon ground cloves

200 g softened butter

1⅓ cups dark brown sugar

3 eggs

fruit cakes

MAKES 18 KEEPS 2 weeks FREEZES 3 months

Wash the dried fruit in a colander under a running tap. Leave to drain for 5 minutes. Put into a bowl with slivered almonds and brandy. Stir to combine and cover with plastic film. Leave to steep overnight if possible.

Preheat oven to 150°C. Line two 12-hole muffin tins with 18 purple cupcake papers.

Sift the flour and spices into a bowl.

In a separate bowl, cream the butter for 1–2 minutes. Add half of the dark brown sugar and beat for 2 minutes. Add remaining sugar and beat for a further 2 minutes or until the sugar has almost dissolved; do not over-beat or you will incorporate too much air.

Add eggs one at a time, beating until just incorporated but not curdled. (If the mixture looks curdled, beat the eggs a little longer between additions or add a tablespoon of plain flour to the mixture.)

continued

FLAVOURING

1 tablespoon marmalade

1 tablespoon raspberry jam

1 tablespoon treacle

1 teaspoon vanilla extract

¼ teaspoon almond essence

1 teaspoon Parisian essence

¼ cup brandy

food colouring: violet and
   Wilton's gooseberry-green

1 kg white fondant

icing sugar, for dusting

7-cm scone cutter

1 egg white

disco violet glitter

18 small mauve sugar roses

18 small hi-lite mauve
   sugar roses

18 small violet sugar roses

purple glitter

1 cup Vanilla Buttercream
   (page 142)

piping bag

leaf tip #66

green glitter

Combine all flavouring ingredients in a jar and screw lid on firmly. Shake to combine thoroughly.

Add the flour mixture to the creamed mixture and beat on low speed until combined. Add the fruit mixture and beat until evenly incorporated. Add the flavouring mixture and beat until thoroughly combined.

Spoon mixture into cupcake papers, filling each to the very top. With a clean wet finger, smooth the top of each cupcake. Bake for 30–40 minutes or until a fine skewer inserted comes out clean. Remove cupcakes from the trays immediately and cool on a wire rack for 1 hour before decorating.

decoration

Add 1 drop of violet food colouring to the ball of fondant and knead until you have a very soft purple colour (see page 15). Dust a work surface with icing sugar and use a rolling pin to roll out the icing into a flat piece 4–5 mm thick. Use the scone cutter to cut out 18 rounds of icing.

Brush each cupcake with egg white and place a round of icing onto each. Use a small brush to lightly dust some disco violet glitter onto the fondant. With a very small brush, paint the tips of each of the sugar roses with egg white and sprinkle with purple glitter. Place three roses (one of each colour) in the centre of each cupcake.

Using a toothpick, add a small amount of the gooseberry-green colouring to the buttercream and mix until you have an even colour. Pipe three leaves of buttercream between the roses (see page 13). Let the buttercream set for about 20 minutes, then use a small brush to apply green glitter to each leaf.

Baby's first cupcakes

Little cupcakes are a big craze at the bakery. We design different ones for celebrations, corporate functions and magazine photo shoots. The baby animal cupcakes are a favourite request for babies' birthdays.

2¾ cups plain flour

2 teaspoons baking powder

200 g softened unsalted butter

1¾ cups castor sugar

6 egg whites

1 teaspoon vanilla extract

1½ teaspoons rose water, violet water or orange blossom water

1 cup milk

scented white cakes

MAKES 48 baby cupcakes or 24 regular cupcakes
KEEPS 2 days FREEZES 2 months

Preheat oven to 170°C. Line four 12-hole mini muffin trays with 24 small pink cupcake papers and 24 small blue cupcake papers.

Sift together the flour and baking powder.

In a separate bowl, cream the butter for 1–2 minutes. Add the castor sugar a third at a time, beating for 2 minutes after each addition. After the last addition, beat until the mixture is light and fluffy and the sugar has almost dissolved. Add egg whites a quarter at a time, beating for 1 minute after each addition or until the mixture is light and fluffy. Add vanilla extract and scented water and beat until combined.

Add a third of the flour mixture to the creamed mixture and beat on low speed until combined. Add half the milk and beat until combined. Repeat this process. Add the remaining third of the flour and beat until thoroughly combined; do not over-beat as this will toughen the mixture.

continued

Divide the mixture evenly between the 48 cupcake papers. Bake for 13 minutes only. Remove cupcakes from the trays immediately and cool on a wire rack for 30 minutes before frosting.

TO MAKE REGULAR CUPCAKES
If using regular cupcake papers instead of small papers, this recipe will make 24 cupcakes. Bake at 170°C for 18–20 minutes or until a skewer inserted comes out clean.

1⅓ quantities Vanilla
   Buttercream (page 142)

food colouring: pink and blue

piping bag

star tip #7

pastel sprinkles

48 sugar animals

decoration

Divide the buttercream into two bowls. Add a couple of drops of pink colouring to one bowl, and a couple of drops of blue to the other. Mix until frosting is evenly coloured.

For the cupcakes in pink papers, pipe pink buttercream onto each cupcake in a circular motion starting around the edge of the cupcake, to create a soft-serve ice-cream effect. Top with sprinkles and a sugar animal.

Repeat this process with the blue buttercream for the cupcakes in blue papers.

afternoon tea cupcakes

I wasn't allowed to drink coffee when I was young but I always loved the flavour of this fluffy coffee and walnut cake. It's even better now that I've turned it into a cupcake and frosted it with Coffee Buttercream. The perfect afternoon pick-me-up.

1½ cups self-raising flour

1 teaspoon baking powder

200 g softened butter

1 cup castor sugar

4 eggs

2 teaspoons vanilla extract

2 tablespoons instant
  coffee granules

¼ cup boiling water

1½ cups chopped walnuts

coffee and walnut cakes

MAKES 24 KEEPS 2 days FREEZES 2 months

Preheat oven to 170°C. Line two 12-hole muffin trays with cupcake papers.

Sift together the flour and baking powder.

In a separate bowl, cream the butter for 1–2 minutes. Add half the castor sugar and beat for 2 minutes. Add the remaining castor sugar and beat for a further 2 minutes or until the mixture is light and fluffy. Add eggs one at a time, beating for 1 minute after each addition or until mixture is light and fluffy. Add the vanilla and beat until combined.

Add half the flour mixture to the creamed mixture and beat on low speed until combined. Dissolve coffee in the boiling water. Add to the cake mixture and beat until dissolved. Add remaining flour and beat until combined; do not over-beat as this will toughen the mixture. Fold in the chopped walnuts.

continued

Spoon mixture into cupcake papers, filling each about three-quarters full. Bake for 18–20 minutes or until a fine skewer inserted comes out clean. Remove cupcakes from the trays immediately and cool on a wire rack for 30 minutes before frosting.

1 quantity Vanilla Buttercream
   (page 142)

2 tablespoons instant coffee
   granules, dissolved in
   1 teaspoon hot water

72 small ivory sugar roses

72 sugar leaves

gold cachous

decoration

Add the coffee to the buttercream and mix until you have an even colour.

Using a round-edged kitchen knife, apply the buttercream in the Crabapple signature swirl (see page 12). Decorate each cupcake with a cluster of three sugar roses, three sugar leaves and some gold cachous.

simnel cupcakes with marzipan

This is an old-fashioned Easter cupcake made with dried fruit and covered with marzipan. Traditionally, eleven marzipan balls would be used to decorate each cupcake, representing the eleven 'good' disciples. In this modern version, I use large silver cachous and a chocolate Easter egg instead.

100 g shop-bought marzipan

1½ cups plain flour

1 teaspoon baking powder

1 teaspoon mixed spice

pinch of salt

200 g softened butter

1 cup soft brown sugar

3 eggs

425 g mixed dried fruit, rinsed

2 tablespoons milk

simnel cakes

MAKES 11 KEEPS 4 days FREEZES 2 months

Preheat oven to 170°C. Line a 12-hole muffin tray with 11 cupcake papers.

Roll the marzipan into 11 small balls and set aside.

Sift together the flour, baking powder, mixed spice and salt.

In a separate bowl, cream the butter and sugar until the mixture becomes a lighter colour. Add eggs one at a time, beating for 1 minute after each addition or until well incorporated; do not overbeat.

Add the flour mixture to the creamed mixture and beat on low speed until just combined. Add the fruit and milk and beat until combined.

continued

Put a tablespoon of mixture into each of the cupcake papers, flattening it down with the back of the spoon. Place a marzipan ball on top of the mixture, cover with another tablespoon of mixture and flatten the top. The mixture should completely cover the marzipan balls and almost fill each cupcake paper.

Bake for 25–30 minutes or until a fine skewer inserted comes out clean. Leave the cupcakes to cool for 5 minutes before removing from the tray and cool on a wire rack for a further 45 minutes before decorating.

icing sugar, for dusting

250 g shop-bought marzipan

7-cm scone cutter

1 egg white

132 large silver cachous

11 small solid-chocolate
   Easter eggs

decoration

Dust a work surface with icing sugar and use a rolling pin to roll out the marzipan into a flat piece 4–5 mm thick. Using the scone cutter, cut out 11 rounds of marzipan. Brush each cupcake with egg white and place a marzipan round on top. Place 11 silver cachous balls around the edge of each cupcake and top with a chocolate Easter egg.

flower power cupcakes

I was brought up in the 1960s and 70s, when 'flower power' was at its height. I was too young to partake in all the activities, but I do remember the crazy colours and oversized designs. The zucchini cake is moist and healthy – the perfect choice to represent the era of all things nat-u-rale.

2 cups plain flour

2 cups wholemeal flour

1 teaspoon salt

3 teaspoons baking powder

1½ teaspoons bicarbonate
   of soda

3 teaspoons ground cinnamon

1 teaspoon ground nutmeg

1 teaspoon ground ginger

1 cup chopped raisins

⅓ cup rum

2 cups vegetable oil

2 cups white sugar

⅔ cup soft brown sugar

6 eggs

5 cups grated zucchini

2 teaspoons vanilla extract

zucchini cakes

MAKES 24 KEEPS 2 days FREEZES 2 months

Preheat oven to 180°C. Line two 12-hole muffin trays with brightly coloured cupcake papers.

Sift together all dry ingredients, except sugars. In a separate bowl, soak the raisins in the rum.

In another bowl, use an electric mixture on medium speed to beat together the oil, sugars and eggs until thick and creamy (about 5 minutes). Add the grated zucchini, rum and raisin mixture, and vanilla and beat on low speed until combined.

Add the flour mixture and beat until thoroughly combined; do not over-beat as this will toughen the mixture.

Spoon mixture into cupcake papers, filling each about three-quarters full. Bake for 20 minutes or until a fine skewer inserted comes out clean. Remove cupcakes from the trays immediately and cool on a wire rack for 30 minutes before frosting.

continued

1 quantity Cream Cheese
Frosting (page 149)
or Vanilla Buttercream
(page 142)

food colouring: your favourite
bright colours

piping bag

star tip #13

green, pink, yellow and
orange nonpareils

24 large sugar flowers

decoration

Divide the frosting into four or five bowls and add enough
food colouring to each to make a different bright colour.
Pipe frosting in a circular motion, starting around the edge
of the cupcake, to form a soft-serve ice-cream effect. Top
with nonpareils and place a sugar flower in the centre of each
cupcake.

VARIATION

If zucchini cupcakes just aren't your thing, you can use this
decoration on Crabapple Bakery's Vanilla Cakes (page 25)
instead.

Nutella shard cupcakes

This hazelnut cake is a nutty version of the Crabapple Bakery Vanilla Cake, and is loved by both children and adults. Partnered with the Nutella Frosting, it's great for an 18th or 21st birthday party – the Frangelico liqueur makes it feel all grown up, while the Nutella appeals to the child within. Alternatively, try frosting with Chocolate Fudge Frosting, Vanilla Buttercream, Chocolate Ganache or Real Caramel Sauce Frosting.

2¾ cups plain flour

2 teaspoons baking powder

½ teaspoon salt

200 g softened unsalted butter

1¾ cups castor sugar

4 eggs

1 tablespoon vanilla extract

1 cup natural yoghurt

½ cup hazelnut meal

hazelnut cakes

MAKES 24 KEEPS 2 days FREEZES 2 months

Preheat oven to 170°C. Line two 12-hole muffin trays with chocolate-coloured cupcake papers.

Sift together the flour, baking powder and salt.

In a separate bowl, cream the butter for 1–2 minutes. Add the castor sugar a third at a time, beating for 2 minutes after each addition. After the last addition, beat until the mixture is light and fluffy and the sugar has almost dissolved. Add eggs one at a time, beating for 1 minute after each addition or until mixture is light and fluffy. Add the vanilla extract and beat until combined.

Add a third of the flour mixture to the creamed mixture and beat on low speed until combined. Add half of the yoghurt and beat until combined. Repeat this process. Add the remaining third of the flour and beat until thoroughly combined; do not over-beat as this will toughen the mixture. Add the hazelnut meal and beat until combined.

continued

Spoon mixture into cupcake papers, filling each about three-quarters full. Bake for 18–20 minutes or until a fine skewer inserted comes out clean. Remove cupcakes from the trays immediately and cool on a wire rack for 30 minutes before frosting.

2 quantities Nutella Frosting (page 153)

piping bag

star tip #11

1 quantity Hazelnut Toffee Shards (page 162)

gold cachous

decoration

Pipe frosting in a circular motion, starting around the edge of the cupcake, to form a soft-serve ice-cream effect. Decorate each cupcake with a toffee shard and some gold cachous.

sweetheart mini cakes

These pretty cakes are perfect for gift giving. They also make a romantic dessert at an engagement party.

1½ cups plain flour

1 tablespoon baking powder

3 cups almond meal

250 g softened unsalted butter

1½ cups castor sugar

6 eggs

1 tablespoon vanilla extract

¼ cup natural yoghurt

almond and vanilla cakes

MAKES 18 mini-heart cakes or 24 regular cupcakes
KEEPS 2 days FREEZES 2 months

Preheat oven to 160°C. Lightly grease three six-hole mini-heart cake trays.

Sift together the flour and baking powder. Add the almond meal and combine.

In a separate bowl, cream the butter for 1–2 minutes. Add half the sugar and beat for 2 minutes. Add the rest of the sugar and beat for a further 2 minutes or until light and fluffy. Add the eggs two at a time, beating for 2 minutes after each addition or until mixture is light and fluffy. Add the vanilla and beat until combined.

Add a third of the flour to the creamed mixture and beat on low speed until combined. Add half of the yoghurt and beat until combined. Repeat this process. Add the remaining third of the flour and beat until thoroughly combined; do not over-beat as this will toughen the mixture.

continued

Spoon mixture into the cake trays, filling each heart just over half full. Bake for 15 minutes or until a fine skewer inserted comes out clean. Leave to cool for about 5 minutes before turning out onto a wire rack to cool for a further 30 minutes before icing.

TO MAKE REGULAR CUPCAKES
If using regular cupcake papers instead of mini-heart trays, this recipe makes 24 cupcakes. Bake at 160°C for 20–25 minutes or until a skewer inserted comes out clean.

2 quantities Quick Royal Icing (page 144)

rose essence

food colouring: rose-pink

1 quantity Sugared Rose Petals (page 162)

decoration

Prepare the icing to pouring consistency. Add 2–3 drops rose essence and 3–4 drops pink food colouring during preparation.

Place the sweetheart cakes onto a fine wire rack with feet. Pour over most of the icing, so that each cake is completely covered. Add a few more drops of the pink food colouring to the remaining icing to create a mid-pink colour. Using a teaspoon, drizzle the icing over so that it runs down the sides a little. Use an offset palette knife to lift the cakes onto a serving plate, then sprinkle with the sugared rose petals.

VARIATION
If you're making these cakes for a man, ice with Dark Chocolate Ganache (page 151) and top with chocolate truffles.

caramel lovers' cupcakes

If you are a caramel lover, then this cupcake is just for you. Made with Real Caramel Sauce and topped with Real Caramel Sauce Frosting, it is bursting with caramel.

3⅓ cups plain flour

3 teaspoons baking powder

1⅓ cups Real Caramel Sauce (page 161)

⅔ cups water

150 g softened butter

1¾ cups castor sugar

4 eggs

caramel cakes

MAKES 24 KEEPS 2 days FREEZES 2 months

Preheat oven to 170°C. Line two 12-hole muffin trays with cupcake papers.

Sift flour and baking powder together.

In a separate bowl whisk together the Real Caramel Sauce and water until well combined.

In another bowl, cream the butter for 1–2 minutes. Add the castor sugar a third at a time, beating for 2 minutes after each addition. After the last addition, beat until the mixture is light and fluffy and the sugar has almost dissolved. Add eggs one at a time, beating for 1 minute after each addition or until mixture is light and fluffy.

Add a third of the flour mixture to the creamed mixture and beat on low speed until combined. Add half of the caramel mixture and beat until combined. Repeat this process. Add the remaining third of the flour and beat until thoroughly combined; do not over-beat as this will toughen the mixture.

continued

Spoon mixture into cupcake papers, filling each to just over half full (this mixture rises a lot). Bake for 18 minutes or until a fine skewer inserted comes out clean. Remove cupcakes from the trays immediately and cool on a wire rack for 30 minutes before frosting.

1 quantity Real Caramel Sauce Frosting (page 147)

24 caramel-filled chocolates, halved

½ cup Real Caramel Sauce (page 161)

decoration

Using a round-edged kitchen knife, apply the frosting to the cupcakes in the Crabapple signature swirl (see page 12). Top each cupcake with a caramel-filled chocolate and use a tablespoon to drizzle over some Real Caramel Sauce.

Rapunzel tower cakes

There is nothing nicer than an apple and vanilla cake, especially when you add the flavours of cloves and cinnamon. I imagine that apples have been used in cakes as far back as medieval times, so although this cake recipe is delicious as a simple cupcake, here I've gone for a bit of a medieval theme. These romantic cakes are extremely popular for weddings.

3 cups plain flour

2 teaspoons baking powder

1 teaspoon bicarbonate of soda

1½ teaspoons ground cinnamon

½ teaspoon ground cloves

½ teaspoon salt

200 g softened unsalted butter

1¾ cups soft brown sugar

4 eggs

1 tablespoon vanilla extract

2 cups Apple Sauce Filling (page 161), pureed until smooth

apple sauce cakes

MAKES 18 darioles or 24 cupcakes
KEEPS 2 days FREEZES 2 months

Preheat oven to 170°C. Lightly grease 18 dariole moulds.

Sift together the flour, baking powder, bicarbonate of soda, cinnamon, cloves and salt.

In a separate bowl, cream the butter for 1–2 minutes. Add the sugar a third at a time, beating for 2 minutes after each addition. After the last addition, beat until the mixture is light and fluffy and the sugar has almost dissolved. Add eggs one at a time, beating for 1 minute after each addition or until mixture is light and fluffy. Add the vanilla extract and beat until combined.

Add half of the flour mixture to the creamed mixture and beat on low speed until combined. Add the remaining flour mixture and beat until thoroughly combined and there are no lumps; do not over-beat as this will toughen the mixture. Add the apple sauce and beat until thoroughly combined.

continued

Spoon mixture into the dariole moulds, filling each about three-quarters full. Bake for 18–20 minutes or until a fine skewer inserted comes out clean. Leave to cool for about 10 minutes before removing from the moulds. Stand cakes upside down on a wire rack to cool for a further 30 minutes before decorating.

TO MAKE REGULAR CUPCAKES

If using regular cupcake papers instead of dariole moulds, this recipe makes 24 cupcakes. Bake at 170°C for 18–20 minutes or until a skewer inserted comes out clean.

decoration

Using a sharp knife, cut the top off each cake to create a flat surface. Pour the icing sugar out onto a short-sided lamington tray and level out. Roll each cake in icing sugar to completely cover the sides.

Using a toothpick, add a small amount of the moss-green colouring to 1 cup of the buttercream and mix until you have an even colour. Pipe four leaves of moss-green buttercream on top of each cake (see page 13). Top nine of the cakes with a mauve sugar daisy.

Add a couple of drops of violet food colouring to the remaining buttercream and mix until you have an even colour. Fill the cleaned piping bag with the purple buttercream and pipe four leaves on top of each of the remaining nine cakes, as pictured. Top each of these cakes with a lemon sugar daisy and place a gold cachous onto each of the green leaves.

2 cups icing sugar

1½ cups Vanilla Buttercream (page 142)

food colouring: violet and Wilton's moss-green

piping bag

leaf tip #66

9 mauve sugar daisies

9 lemon sugar daisies

gold cachous

Alice in Wonderland cupcakes

When I first started my cupcake business all I wanted to produce was an Alice in Wonderland cupcake. It had to be pink and white and contain coconut. It wasn't easy, but after a few false starts, I finally created the perfect coconut cake, frosted it with pink coconut ice and topped it with a glacé cherry. I had my Alice in Wonderland Cupcake.

2¼ cups plain flour

1½ teaspoons baking powder

¾ cup desiccated coconut

⅔ cup milk

400 g sour cream

200 g softened butter

½ teaspoon coconut essence

1½ cups castor sugar

3 eggs

1 cup chopped glacé cherries

coconut and cherry cakes

MAKES 24 KEEPS 2 days FREEZES 2 months

Preheat oven to 160°C. Line two 12-hole muffin trays with bright pink cupcake papers.

Sift together the flour and baking powder. Add the desiccated coconut and mix through using your hands.

In a separate bowl, mix the milk and sour cream until smooth.

In another bowl, cream the butter and coconut essence for 1–2 minutes. Add the castor sugar a third at a time, beating for 2 minutes after each addition. After the last addition, beat until the mixture is light and fluffy and the sugar has almost dissolved.

Add eggs one at a time, beating for 1 minute after each addition or until mixture is light and fluffy.

continued

Add a third of the flour mixture to the creamed mixture and beat on low speed until combined. Add half of the sour cream mixture and beat until just combined. Repeat this process. Add the remaining third of the flour and beat until thoroughly combined; do not over-beat as this will toughen the mixture. Add the glacé cherries and beat until just combined.

Spoon mixture into cupcake papers, filling each about half full. Bake for 18–20 minutes or until a fine skewer inserted comes out clean. Remove cupcakes from the trays immediately and cool on a wire rack for 30 minutes before frosting.

1 quantity Coconut Ice
  Frosting (page 149)

1 cup desiccated coconut

12 glacé cherries, halved

decoration

The Coconut Ice Frosting sets very quickly and must be used as soon as it is ready. Use your hands to roll a large spoonful of icing into a ball about the size of a peach. Place the ball on top of the cupcake and shape with your hands to create a dome. Immediately cover the coconut ice with desiccated coconut and top with half a cherry.

all year round gingerbread cupcakes

I adapted this recipe from an American version when I was searching for a Christmastime gingerbread cupcake that would be enjoyed by children and adults alike. This is a cupcake you can enjoy all year round.

2 cups plain flour

¼ teaspoon bicarbonate of soda

¼ teaspoon salt

1½ teaspoons ground ginger

½ teaspoon ground nutmeg

⅛ teaspoon allspice

150 g softened unsalted butter

1¾ cups castor sugar

4 eggs

1½ teaspoons vanilla extract

2 teaspoons grated fresh ginger (optional)

⅔ cup sour cream

⅓ cup finely chopped crystallised ginger

¾ cup finely chopped walnuts

gingerbread cakes

MAKES 24 KEEPS 2 days FREEZES 2 months

Preheat oven to 170°C. Line two 12-hole muffin trays with orange cupcake papers.

Sift together flour, bicarbonate of soda, salt, ground ginger, nutmeg and allspice.

In a separate bowl, cream the butter for 1–2 minutes. Add the castor sugar a third at a time, beating for 2 minutes after each addition. After the last addition, beat until the mixture is light and fluffy and the sugar has almost dissolved.

Add eggs one at a time, beating for 1 minute after each addition or until mixture is light and fluffy. Add the vanilla and grated ginger and combine well.

continued

Add a third of the flour mixture to the creamed mixture and beat on low speed until combined. Add half of the sour cream and beat until combined. Repeat this process. Add the remaining third of the flour and beat until thoroughly combined; do not over-beat as this will toughen the mixture. Add the crystallised ginger and walnuts and stir in.

Spoon mixture into cupcake papers, filling each about three-quarters full. Bake for 20 minutes or until a fine skewer inserted comes out clean. Remove cupcakes from the trays immediately and cool on a wire rack for 30 minutes before frosting

1 quantity Vanilla Buttercream (page 142)

24 sugar gingerbread men

red, yellow and white nonpareils (or sprinkles)

decoration

Using a round-edged kitchen knife, apply the buttercream in the Crabapple signature swirl (see page 12). Working quickly, before the buttercream dries, decorate each cupcake with a sugar gingerbread man and sprinkle with nonpareils.

layer cakes

vanilla fairy birthday cake with cupcakes

A Vanilla Cake with Vanilla Buttercream is probably the most old-fashioned cake you can serve, and it surpasses even the sponge when it comes to birthdays. Our most popular request is this Vanilla Fairy Birthday Cake, for all the little (and big!) birthday girls out there.

1 quantity Crabapple Bakery's Vanilla Cakes mixture (page 25)

vanilla fairy layer cake

KEEPS 2 days

Preheat oven to 170°C. Lightly grease two 23-cm round cake tins.

Divide Vanilla Cakes mixture between the two cake tins. Bake for 35 minutes, or until a skewer inserted comes out clean.

continued

1 egg white

6 purple rose candles

glitter

1 sugar butterfly

assorted large and small
   sugar flowers

1 quantity Vanilla Buttercream
   (page 142)

food colouring: pink

25-cm silver cake round

1 quantity Strawberries and
   Cream filling (page 154)

piping bag

round tip #9

round tip #5

1 large fairy

2 small fairies

pink and silver cachous

1½ metres purple ribbon

filling and decoration

With a small brush, paint a little egg white around the tips of the candles and sprinkle with glitter. Sprinkle glitter on to the sugar butterfly and some of the sugar flowers.

Add several drops of pink food colouring to the buttercream, and mix until you have an even colour. Fill the cake with the Strawberries and Cream filling (step 1 on page 16). Crumbcoat and frost the cake with three-quarters of the buttercream (steps 2–3 on page 16).

Put the remaining buttercream into a piping bag with the #9 round tip attached and pipe six blobs of filling along one edge of the top of the cake. Place a candle into each blob. Using the round tip #5, pipe smaller blobs of buttercream all around the base of the cake.

Position the large fairy and two smaller fairies on the back third of the cake. Decorate the top and sides of the cake with an assortment of flowers, the butterfly, and pink and silver cachous. Wrap the ribbon around the cake, tying with a bow in the front.

vanilla fairy cupcakes

24 Crabapple Bakery's Vanilla Cakes (page 25) – 12 in pink papers and 12 in purple papers

1 quantity Vanilla Buttercream (page 142)

food colouring:
   pink and mauve

8 large sugar flowers

green sugar leaves

pink cachous

8 small fairies

silver cachous

8 sugar butterflies

small sugar flowers

green sprinkles

decoration

Divide the buttercream into two bowls. Add a couple of drops of pink colouring to one bowl, and a couple of drops of mauve to the other. Mix until you have even colours.

Using a round-edged kitchen knife, apply the pink buttercream to the cupcakes in the pink papers using the Crabapple signature swirl (see page 12). Repeat with the mauve buttercream for the cupcakes in purple papers.

Divide the cupcakes into three groups, with even numbers of pink and purple cupcakes in each. For the first group, place a large sugar flower on top of each cupcake, then add two green leaves and a couple of pink cachous. For the second group, place a fairy on top of each cupcake and sprinkle with silver cachous.

For the last group, place a butterfly in the middle of each cupcake, with a couple of small sugar flowers and some green sugar leaves around it. Sprinkle edges with green sprinkles.

over-the-top
passionfruit sponge

If you were brought up on the land, like I was, passionfruit sponges were probably one of your family's staple desserts. Being an over-the-top sort of girl, I have stayed true to myself with this three-layer sponge filled with lemon curd, passionfruit sauce and whipped cream. I hope you love it as much as I do.

6 eggs

1 cup castor sugar

½ cup plain flour

½ cup self-raising flour

¼ cup cornflour

¼ cup custard powder

sponge layer cake

KEEPS 2 days FREEZES 2 weeks

Preheat oven to 170°C. Lightly grease three 20-cm round layer-cake tins.

Beat the eggs for 1 minute using an electric mixer on medium speed. Beat for a further 15 minutes on high speed. Gradually add the sugar, beating after each addition until dissolved. Once you have added all the sugar, beat for a further 10 minutes, until light and fluffy.

Combine the flours and custard powder by sifting together three times. Using a slotted metal spoon, fold the flour mixture into the egg mixture until just combined.

Divide the mixture evenly between the three tins. Bake for 20 minutes, or until the sponges have come away from the sides of the tins. Remove from the tins immediately and cool on a wire rack for 30 minutes before filling.

continued

25-cm silver cake round

2 cups whipped cream

piping bag

star tip #11

½ cup Rich Tangy Lemon Curd
    Filling (page 157)

¼ cup Passionfruit Sauce
    (page 160)

1 quantity Passionfruit Icing
    (page 148)

gold cachous

2 thin skewers

fresh strawberries, halved

4 oriental lilies

filling and decoration

Place one of the sponges onto the silver cake round. Place half of the whipped cream into the piping bag with star tip attached, and pipe large cream rosettes around the outside edge of the sponge. Pour half of the lemon curd onto the top of the sponge and spread over with a small offset palette knife. Pipe some more cream rosettes over the lemon curd to create a flat surface for the next layer to sit on. Using a table-spoon, drizzle some Passionfruit Sauce over the whipped cream rosettes.

Place a second sponge layer on top and repeat this proc-ess with the rest of the lemon curd, cream and Passionfruit Sauce.

Using a large offset palette knife, spread the passionfruit icing over the top of the third sponge layer, allowing some of the icing to dribble over the sides. Sprinkle with gold cachous. Place this final layer on top of the previous two.

Cut the skewers to the height of the layer cake, then push each skewer down through the cake to secure the layers in place. Cover the holes where the skewers were inserted with a little passionfruit icing.

Push the strawberry halves, flat-side down, into the filling between each layer, leaving a little of each strawberry pok-ing out.

Top the cake with the oriental lilies.

ginger fluff sponge with apple sauce filling

This is not just another sponge cake. For one thing, it keeps really well. For another, it tastes sensational – especially when partnered with Apple Sauce Filling. Wrapped in sponge fingers and tied with a big bow, this layer cake looks amazing too.

⅓ cup self-raising flour

⅓ cup cornflour

3 teaspoons ground ginger

1 teaspoon ground cinnamon

2 teaspoons cocoa

5 eggs, separated

¾ cup castor sugar

1 tablespoon golden syrup

ginger fluff sponge layer cake

KEEPS 4 days FREEZES 2 weeks

Preheat oven to 190°C. Grease two 20-cm round layer-cake tins.

Combine the flours, spices and cocoa by sifting together three times.

Using an electric mixer on high speed, beat the egg whites until soft peaks form. Gradually add the sugar, beating after each addition until dissolved. Add the egg yolks and golden syrup and beat until well combined.

Using a slotted metal spoon, fold the sifted flour mixture into the egg mixture until just combined.

Divide the mixture evenly between the two cake tins. Bake for 13 minutes or until the sponges have come away from the sides of the tins. Remove from the tins immediately and cool on a wire rack for 30 minutes before filling.

continued

25-cm silver cake round

3 cups whipped cream

piping bag

star tip #11

½ cup Apple Sauce Filling
(page 161)

1 × 250-g packet thin
sponge fingers

1 metre pink ribbon

6 gingernut biscuits, crushed

fresh roses

icing sugar, for dusting

glitter

filling and decoration

Cut the tops off each sponge using a bread knife, to create a flat top.

Place one of the sponges onto the silver cake round. Put half of the whipped cream into the piping bag with star tip attached, and pipe large rosettes around the edge of the top of the cake. Pour the apple sauce over this layer, spreading it with a small offset palette knife. Pipe some more cream rosettes over the apple sauce to create a flat surface for the next layer to sit on. Place the second sponge upside down on top of the first.

Using a large offset palette knife, spread a thin layer of whipped cream over the sides of the sponge. Stick the sponge fingers like fence palings to the sides of the sponge until completely covered. Tie the ribbon around the cake, making a big bow at the front.

Using the palette knife, spread the remaining whipped cream on top of the sponge. Sprinkle with the crushed biscuits and decorate with the roses. Dust with icing sugar and sprinkle with glitter.

you're a star cake

You don't have to wait for a birthday, christening or anniversary to make a beautiful cake. Sometimes it's fun to give a cake to someone just to let them know that you think they're a star.

1 quantity Chocolate Birthday Cakes mixture (page 27)

chocolate birthday layer cake

KEEPS 2 days

Preheat oven to 170°C. Lightly grease two 20-cm round cake tins.

Divide the Chocolate Birthday Cakes mixture between the two cake tins. Bake for 35 minutes, or until a skewer inserted comes out clean.

continued

1 quantity Vanilla Buttercream (page 142)

food colouring: violet

25-cm silver cake round

1 cup Chocolate Mousse and Honeycomb Filling (page 158)

3 piping bags

star tip #9

1 sheet baking paper

round tip #4

1 cup white chocolate pieces, melted

yellow chocolate oil colour

5 lengths white florists wire

gold lustre dust

gold glitter

red chocolate oil colour

round tip #2

gold cachous

filling and decoration

Add about 20–30 drops of violet food colouring to the buttercream to make a dark purple frosting.

Fill the cake with the chocolate mousse filling (step 1 on page 16). Crumbcoat and frost the cake with three-quarters of the buttercream (steps 2–3 on page 16). Put the remaining buttercream into a piping bag with the star tip attached and pipe eight blobs of icing evenly around the edge of the top of the cake.

On the baking paper use a pencil to draw 12 small stars, 11 medium stars and one large star. Turn the baking paper over. Add a few drops of yellow oil to the melted chocolate and mix to create an even colour. Fill a piping bag with the round tip #4 attached with most of the melted chocolate. Trace the outline of each star with the chocolate, then fill them in. Wind three-quarters of each length of florists wire around a pencil so that it forms a spiral. Lay the uncurled end of the wire across a medium star while the chocolate is still wet. Repeat this process on two more medium stars and two small stars. Place all of the stars in the fridge to set for around 5 minutes.

When the stars are set, turn them over to expose the flat underside. Use a small brush to apply some gold lustre dust to all but the largest star. Sprinkle all of the stars with gold glitter. Colour the remaining melted chocolate with a few drops of red oil. Fill a piping bag with the round tip #2 attached and write 'You're a Star' on the large chocolate star. Position this in the centre of the cake. Place eight medium-sized stars on each of the blobs and ten small stars around the sides of the cake. Arrange the five wired stars behind the large central star. Sprinkle over the gold cachous.

congratulations layer cake

There is no better way to congratulate someone than with a beautiful layer cake that you have made yourself. This cake is sure to be a knockout – don't be surprised if people end up congratulating you!

1 quantity White Chocolate
Mud Cakes mixture
(page 33)

white chocolate mud layer cake

KEEPS 3 days

Preheat oven to 170°C. Lightly grease two 20-cm square cake tins.

Divide White Chocolate Mud Cakes mixture between the two cake tins. Bake for 45 minutes, or until a skewer inserted comes out clean.

continued

25-cm gold or silver
  cake board

1 cup Baileys Irish Cream
  Filling with Maltesers
  (page 160)

1 quantity White Chocolate
  Ganache (page 152)

2 piping bags

round tip #5

round tip #9

26 Belgian chocolate seashells

½ cup white chocolate
  pieces, melted

plastic margarine lid (round)

½ cup dark chocolate
  pieces, melted

round tip #2

gold cachous

1 metre chocolate-coloured
  ribbon

filling and decoration

Fill the cake with the Bailey's filling (step 1 on page 16). Crumb-coat and frost the cake with three-quarters of the ganache (steps 2–3 on page 16).

Put the remaining ganache in a piping bag with the round tip #5 attached and pipe small blobs all the way around the base of the cake. Using the piping bag with round tip #9 attached, pipe 16 larger blobs of ganache around the edge of the top of the cake, and ten around the sides. Place a chocolate sea-shell on each blob.

To make the plaque, pour the melted white chocolate into the top of the margarine lid and leave to set in the refrig-erator for about 15 minutes. Once set, remove the plaque from the lid and turn over to expose the flat underside. Put the melted dark chocolate into a piping bag with the round tip #2 attached and write 'Congratulations' on the plaque. You can pipe a design around the edge if you wish. Position the plaque in the centre of the cake. Sprinkle gold cachous over the cake.

Wrap the ribbon around the bottom of the cake, using melted dark chocolate to keep it in place.

frostings & fillings

guide to making flavoured and coloured buttercream

This table assumes you have 1 quantity of Vanilla Buttercream Frosting.

NAME	FLAVOURING	FOOD COLOURING
Apricot	2–3 drops apricot essence	4–5 drops perfect peach
Coconut Cream	use coconut milk instead of milk when making buttercream	none
Coffee	2 tablespoons instant coffee granules dissolved in 1 teaspoon hot water	none
Ghoulish	none	10–15 drops of any dark colour
Girlish	none	2–3 drops of any pastel colour
Lavender	2–3 drops culinary lavender oil	2–3 drops violet
Lemon Blossom	use lemon juice instead of milk when making buttercream	2–3 drops yellow
Musk	2–3 drops musk essence	3–4 drops baby pink
Peach Blossom	2–3 drops peach essence	2–3 drops perfect peach
Peppermint	2–3 drops peppermint essence	4–5 drops baby blue
Raspberry	2–3 drops raspberry essence	6–7 drops raspberry
Rose Petal	2–3 drops rose essence	3–4 drops rose pink
Spearmint	2–3 drops spearmint essence	2–3 drops emerald green
Strawberry	2–3 drops strawberry essence	4–5 drops raspberry
Violet	2–3 drops violet essence	5–6 drops violet

vanilla buttercream frosting

This buttercream frosting is very light and creamy. At the bakery this is our most popular frosting. Use the guide on the previous page to create a variety of flavours and colours.

200 g softened unsalted butter

½ cup milk

1 tablespoon vanilla extract

8 cups icing sugar

MAKES 4 cups of frosting – enough for 24 cupcakes
KEEPS 1 week

Cream the butter for 1–2 minutes. Add the milk, vanilla extract and half of the sifted icing sugar, and beat for at least 3 minutes or until the mixture is light and fluffy. Add the remaining icing sugar and beat for a further 3 minutes or until the mixture is light and fluffy and of a spreadable consistency. Add extra milk if the mixture is too dry or extra icing sugar if the mixture is too wet.

If you wish to colour and/or flavour the buttercream then this is the time to do it (except for lemon blossom and coconut – see guide on previous page). Follow the guide on the previous page to create the colours and flavours you desire. Add a drop at a time and beat in until you reach the required colour and/or flavour.

chocolate fudge frosting

This is the first frosting I learnt how to make in home economics at high school. I still think it has the greatest flavour and it can be used with a wide variety of cupcakes. The Banana Fudge Cupcake is a personal favourite of my daughter Natalie, who is in charge of making all the frostings at the bakery.

8 cups icing sugar

1 cup cocoa

200 g softened butter

¾ cup milk

1 tablespoon vanilla extract

MAKES 4 cups frosting – enough for 24 cupcakes

KEEPS 1 week

Sift the icing sugar and cocoa into a bowl.

In a separate bowl, cream the butter for 1–2 minutes. Add the milk, vanilla extract and half of the icing sugar mixture, and beat for at least 3 minutes or until the mixture is light and fluffy. Add the remaining icing sugar and beat for a further 3 minutes or until the mixture is light and fluffy and of a spreadable consistency. Add extra milk if the mixture is too dry or extra icing sugar if the mixture is too wet.

You can use this frosting immediately.

quick royal icing

I have to confess I hate making royal icing from scratch because it's so messy, so I was delighted when I came upon a premix royal icing mixture. I use this icing for dipping cupcakes, writing on plaques, and drizzling over darioles and gingerbread cakes. It's also fantastic for fine line decoration on smooth-iced cupcakes, as it sets hard and opaque.

water

500-g bag premix royal icing

MAKES ¾ cup icing – enough for 12 cupcakes

KEEPS Does not keep. Use immediately

Simply add a little water at a time to the sifted icing sugar, until you have the required consistency. If you want to use a flavouring essence, add a couple of drops to the icing sugar before you add the water. If you want to use colouring, add it before you reach the desired consistency (if you add it at the end it will thin the icing). Use fruit juice or coconut milk instead of water for a flavoured icing.

simple icing

This icing is simple, tastes great, and can be easily coloured and flavoured. Use it on almost any cupcake as an icing, or thin it down to use as a glaze for cupcakes that don't require any more sweetness. This icing is softer and more transparent than the Quick Royal Icing.

water

4 cups icing sugar

MAKES 1½ cups icing – enough for 24 cupcakes

KEEPS Does not keep. Use immediately

Simply add a little water at a time to the sifted icing sugar, until you have the required consistency. If you want to use a flavouring essence, add a couple of drops to the icing sugar before you add the water. If you want to use colouring, add it before you reach the desired consistency (if you add it at the end it will thin the icing). Use fruit juice or coconut milk instead of water for a flavoured icing.

real caramel sauce frosting

I discovered this frosting while I was making some caramel sauce for my sticky date puddings (I just can't keep my finger out of the pot, even while the sauce is boiling). I decided to boil the sauce for longer to reduce it, and then let it cool to room temperature. I tried adding some icing sugar and before I knew it I had Real Caramel Sauce Frosting.

100 g butter

⅔ cups soft brown sugar

¼ cup golden syrup

½ cup cream

8 cups icing sugar

MAKES 4 cups frosting – enough for 24 cupcakes
KEEPS 1 week

Combine the butter, sugar, golden syrup and cream in a heavy-based saucepan over medium heat. Stir occasionally with a flat-bottomed wooden spoon until the sugar has dissolved. Turn heat up to high and boil for at least 5 minutes. Take off the heat and cool to room temperature.

Add half of the sifted icing sugar to the cooled caramel mixture and use an electric mixer on medium speed to beat for 3 minutes or until the mixture is light and fluffy. Add the remaining icing sugar and beat for a further 3 minutes or until the mixture is light and fluffy and of a spreadable consistency. Add extra cream if the mixture is too dry or extra icing sugar if the mixture is too wet.

You can use this frosting immediately.

passionfruit icing

This is the most popular flavoured icing at the bakery. Passionfruit is probably the oldest and most popular icing flavour for buttercakes and sponges in Australia. I doubt there's an agricultural show in the country that doesn't have a passionfruit sponge, passionfruit small cake or passionfruit yo-yo section.

50 g softened butter

½ cup fresh passionfruit pulp

4 cups icing sugar

MAKES 2 cups icing – enough for 24 cupcakes

KEEPS 1 day. Best used immediately

Combine the butter, passionfruit and half of the sifted icing sugar in a bowl. Stir with a knife until smooth. Gradually add remaining icing sugar and combine until smooth and of spreadable consistency.

orange juice icing

This icing is perfect on our Orange and Poppy Seed Cakes. If you prefer a strong orange flavour try adding the zest of half an orange to the mixture.

50 g softened butter

½ cup freshly squeezed orange juice, strained

4 cups icing sugar

MAKES 2 cups icing – enough for 24 cupcakes

KEEPS 1 day. Best used immediately

Combine butter, orange juice and half of the sifted icing sugar in a bowl. Stir with a knife until smooth. Gradually add remaining icing sugar and combine until smooth and of a spreadable consistency.

cream cheese frosting

125 g softened unsalted
   butter

400 g softened cream cheese

1½ teaspoons vanilla extract

6 cups icing sugar

MAKES 4 cups frosting – enough for 24 cupcakes
KEEPS 4 days

Cream the butter for 1–2 minutes. Add the cream cheese, vanilla and half of the sifted icing sugar and beat for 3 minutes or until the mixture is light and fluffy. Gradually add remaining icing sugar and beat until the mixture is light and fluffy and of a spreadable consistency. You can use the frosting immediately.

coconut ice frosting

This frosting was adapted from my Pink Coconut Ice recipe. Unfortunately, the coconut ice mixture doesn't spread, but I found that I could mould it onto a cupcake while the mixture was still warm.

9 egg whites

6 cups desiccated coconut

9 cups icing sugar

food colouring: pink

MAKES Enough frosting for 24 cupcakes
KEEPS Does not keep. Use immediately

Beat the egg whites for 15 seconds using an electric mixer on low speed. Add coconut, sifted icing sugar and 3–4 drops of pink colouring, and beat until just combined.

This frosting sets very quickly and must be used immediately. If you have any mixture left over you can keep it to eat as coconut ice.

marshmallow frosting

This is the most time consuming frosting to make and unfortunately you can't keep it because it sets, but our customers love it. It is great on cupcakes, birthday cakes and wedding cakes.

3 egg whites

480 g white sugar

3 teaspoons light corn syrup

¼ teaspoon cream of tartar

150 ml water

¾ teaspoon vanilla extract

food colouring: pink

MAKES Enough frosting for 24 cupcakes
KEEPS Does not keep. Use immediately

In a metal bowl combine the egg whites, sugar, corn syrup, cream of tartar and water. Place the bowl over a saucepan of simmering water (making sure the bottom of the bowl does not touch the water) and beat continuously with a hand-held electric mixer until the mixture is light and fluffy and forms soft peaks. Take the bowl off the heat and add the vanilla and a few drops of pink food colouring. Whisk the mixture until it forms stiff peaks.

dark chocolate ganache

It's impossible to get this recipe wrong. Any combination of cream and chocolate will work – the proportions just depend on what the ganache will be used for. If you want it for a chocolate sauce, add more cream. If you want to use it for frosting, add extra chocolate. If you want it a little fudgier, just add some butter. Easy!

1½ cups cream

400 g dark cooking chocolate, chopped

MAKES 3 cups frosting – enough for 24 cupcakes
KEEPS 1 week

In a heavy-based saucepan, bring the cream to the boil. Place the chocolate into a bowl and pour the boiling cream over. Leave for 1 minute to soften. Use a small spatula to carefully stir the ganache, being careful not to incorporate any air, until you achieve a silky frosting.

To use: If you want to achieve a smooth surface, dip cupcakes into the frosting immediately. If you want to achieve a fluffy frosting, let the ganache cool to room temperature and then apply to the cupcake with a small spatula. Do not stir the set ganache too much as it will become dull.

white chocolate ganache

This ganache is similar to the Dark Chocolate Ganache, but you don't need to add as much cream, because white chocolate is made primarily of milk, sugar and cocoa butter. White chocolate contains no cocoa solids at all (which is what gives dark chocolate its colour and flavour), so it's not really chocolate at all. Who cares, it still tastes divine.

1 cup cream

600 g white chocolate, chopped

MAKES 3 cups frosting – enough for 24 cupcakes
KEEPS 1 week

In a heavy-based saucepan, bring the cream to the boil. Place the chocolate into a bowl and pour the boiling cream over. Leave for 1 minute to soften. Use a small spatula to carefully stir the ganache, being careful not to incorporate any air, until you achieve a silky frosting.

To use: If you want to achieve a smooth surface, dip cupcakes into the frosting immediately. If you want to achieve a fluffy frosting, let the ganache cool to room temperature and then apply to the cupcake with a small spatula. Do not stir the set ganache too much as it will become dull.

Nutella frosting

I am not a big fan of Nutella myself, but the staff at the bakery insisted that we *must* have a Nutella cupcake. With Frangelico liqueur and whipped cream added to the Nutella, even I enjoy this icing. You can use Tia Maria as an alternative to the Frangelico. You may wish to omit the alcohol if serving to children.

1 750-g jar Nutella

1 tablespoon Frangelico

½ cup whipped cream

MAKES 2½ cups frosting – enough for 12 cupcakes

KEEPS 1 week

Spoon the Nutella into a bowl and stir in the Frangelico. Put the whipped cream into a small bowl and fold in a quarter of the Nutella mixture. Then fold the whipped cream mixture into the remaining Nutella.

cookies and cream filling

It seems people just can't get enough of cookies and cream. It would have to be the most popular birthday cake filling on the planet – well, it's the most popular at our bakery anyway.

1 cup thickened cream

1 tablespoon icing sugar

¼ teaspoon vanilla extract

8 Oreos or chocolate ripple cookies, crushed

MAKES 2 cups of filling KEEPS 2 days

Using an electric mixer with whisk attachment, whisk the cream, icing sugar and vanilla for 1 minute on medium speed. Then turn the speed to high and whisk until stiff. Stir in the crushed cookies.

strawberries and cream filling

1 cup thickened cream

1 tablespoon icing sugar

¼ teaspoon vanilla extract

⅓ cup chopped fresh strawberries

MAKES 2 cups of filling KEEPS 2 days

Using an electric mixer with whisk attachment, whisk the cream, icing sugar and vanilla for 1 minute on medium speed. Then turn the speed to high and whisk until stiff. Stir in the strawberries.

raspberries and cream filling

1 cup thickened cream

1 tablespoon icing sugar

¼ teaspoon vanilla extract

½ cup fresh raspberries

MAKES 2 cups of filling KEEPS 2 days

Using an electric mixer with whisk attachment, whisk the cream, icing sugar and vanilla for 1 minute on medium speed. Then turn the speed to high and whisk until stiff. Stir in the raspberries.

jam and cream filling

When I was a child on the farm, I remember Dad making us jam and fresh cream on bread, as though we were having Devonshire Tea. Jam and cream is still an old-fashioned favourite for filling sponges and layer cakes.

1 cup thickened cream

1 tablespoon icing sugar

½ teaspoon vanilla extract

¼ cup jam, any flavour

MAKES 1½ cups of filling KEEPS 2 days

Using an electric mixer with whisk attachment, whisk the cream, icing sugar and vanilla for 1 minute on medium speed. Then turn the speed to high and whisk until stiff.

Use a fork to stir the jam until smooth. Drop dollops of jam into the cream a little at a time and gently fold through.

rich tangy lemon curd filling

If you are like me and enjoy a lemon tart that is nice and tangy, then you'll love this zesty lemon curd filling.

12 egg yolks

1½ cups white sugar

3 tablespoons lemon zest

250 ml freshly squeezed
    lemon juice

½ teaspoon lemon essence

200 g unsalted butter,
    chopped into small pieces

MAKES 3 cups of filling KEEPS 1 month

Place egg yolks, sugar, and lemon zest, juice and essence into a heavy-based saucepan and whisk together over medium heat until thoroughly combined. Stir continuously with a flat-bottomed wooden spoon until thick and bubbly. Remove from the heat and add the butter a piece at a time, stirring until melted.

Chill the lemon curd in the refrigerator until firm.

lemon curd and cream filling

1 cup thickened cream

1 tablespoon icing sugar

½ teaspoon vanilla extract

¼ cup lemon curd

MAKES 1½ cups of filling KEEPS 2 days

Using an electric mixer with whisk attachment, whisk the cream, icing sugar and vanilla for 1 minute on medium speed. Then turn the speed to high and whisk until stiff. Stir in the lemon curd.

chocolate mousse and honeycomb filling

I can win over any little boy's heart by suggesting a chocolate mousse filling for their special birthday cake. I use a cheat's way of making the mousse, but who said the real way was the right way anyway?

1 cup Dark Chocolate
   Ganache (page 151)

½ cup whipped cream

Crunchie bar, lightly crushed

MAKES 2 cups of filling KEEPS 2 days

Cool the ganache to room temperature and then fold a fork through it to open up the texture. Using a small rubber spatula, fold half of the whipped cream through until just combined. Then fold through the remaining cream. (If you want the mousse to be lighter, just add more whipped cream.) Fold in the crushed Crunchie.

chocolate mousse and Maltesers filling

1 cup Dark Chocolate
   Ganache (page 151)

½ cup whipped cream

1 cup Maltesers, lightly
   crushed

MAKES 2 cups of filling KEEPS 2 days

Cool the ganache to room temperature and then fold a fork through it to open up the texture. Using a small rubber spatula, fold half of the whipped cream through until just combined. Then fold through the remaining cream. (If you want the mousse to be lighter, just add more whipped cream.) Fold in the crushed Maltesers.

my not-so-secret caramel filling

People think I'm a genius when they taste my 'secret' caramel filling. It's my Mum who is actually the genius – once she taught me the recipe she never had to make it herself again.

1 × 440-g tin condensed milk

1 cup whipped cream

MAKES 2 cups of filling KEEPS 2 days

Remove the label from the tin of condensed milk, and place it into a saucepan of boiling water (the water must cover the tin). Boil for 2 hours. You will need to top up the saucepan with more boiling water about every half hour.

Carefully remove the tin from the water using a pair of tongs and place on a wooden board. Place a tin-opener onto the tin but do not puncture it yet or you will end up with caramel all over the walls and ceiling, or worse, burn yourself. Cover the tin and opener with a tea towel – now you can safely puncture the tin to let the pressure out. Remove the tea towel and open up the tin to reveal your caramel.

Pour the caramel into a bowl and cool to room temperature. Fold a fork through the caramel to open up the texture. Using a small spatula, fold half of the whipped cream through until just combined. Fold through the remaining whipped cream.

Baileys Irish Cream filling

Warning: with the amount of Baileys I put in this filling, this recipe is strictly adults only. Don't be afraid to substitute the Baileys for any of your favourite liquors, like Cointreau, Frangelico, hic, Kahlua, hic, oh stop!

1 cup White Chocolate Ganache (page 152)

2 tablespoons Baileys Irish Cream

¼ cup whipped cream

½ cup Maltesers, lightly crushed (optional)

MAKES 1½ cups of filling KEEPS 2 days

Cool the ganache to room temperature and then fold a fork through it to open up the texture. Using a small rubber spatula, fold through the Baileys, followed by half of the whipped cream, until just combined. Then fold through the remaining cream and Maltesers.

passionfruit sauce

I just love this sauce on the Over-the-top Passionfruit Sponge. It doesn't keep very well, so I use any leftovers as a delicious topping on vanilla ice-cream.

⅔ cup passionfruit pulp

¼ cup orange juice

1½ tablespoons castor sugar

3 teaspoons cornflour

2 tablespoons water

MAKES 1 cup of sauce KEEPS 4 days

Combine the passionfruit pulp, orange juice and sugar in a heavy-based saucepan over a medium heat. In a small cup combine the cornflour and water and stir until smooth. Add to the saucepan and stir continuously with a flat-bottomed wooden spoon until thick and bubbly. Chill in the refrigerator until cold.

apple sauce filling

This filling is just perfect for my Ginger Fluff Sponge. It's also delicious as a filling for butterfly cupcakes, served with custard for a simple dessert, or as a sauce with roast pork.

250 g Granny Smith apples, peeled, cored and quartered

juice of ½ a lemon

grated zest of ½ a lemon

½ cup white sugar

1 cinnamon stick

1 teaspoon vanilla extract

MAKES 1 cup of filling KEEPS 1 week

Toss the apple quarters in the lemon juice and set aside. Reserve any excess juice.

In a heavy-based saucepan, combine the reserved lemon juice, lemon zest, sugar and cinnamon stick and heat gently until the sugar has dissolved. Simmer for 2–3 minutes more before adding the apple. Simmer for about 10 minutes or until the apple is just soft and the liquid has reduced. Drain off any excess liquid and place the cooked apples into a bowl with the vanilla. Remove cinnamon stick and mash with a fork until smooth.

real caramel sauce

100 g butter

⅔ cups soft brown sugar

¼ cup golden syrup

½ cup cream

MAKES 1 cup sauce KEEPS 1 month

Combine the butter, sugar, golden syrup and cream in a heavy-based saucepan over medium heat. Stir occasionally with a flat-bottomed wooden spoon until the sugar has dissolved. Turn heat up to high and boil for at least 5 minutes. Take off the heat and cool to room temperature.

sugared rose petals

2 fresh pink rose heads
(that have not been sprayed
with any chemicals)

1 egg white, lightly beaten

castor sugar

Rinse the rose heads under cold water. Gently pat dry. Dip each rose petal into the egg white until just covered. Dip the wet petals into a bowl of fine castor sugar and shake off any excess. Place them on a wire rack to dry for about 1 hour.

hazelnut toffee shards

1 cup chopped roasted
hazelnuts

4 cups castor sugar

2 cups water

MAKES 24 toffee shards

Spread the hazelnuts evenly over a greased baking tray.

In a heavy-based saucepan, heat the sugar and water over a low to medium heat. Stir with a wooden spoon until the sugar has dissolved. Bring to the boil, then reduce the heat and simmer until the mixture turns golden brown. Remove from the heat and allow mixture to settle for a few minutes, until it becomes clear.

Pour the toffee over the hazelnuts (don't scrape the bowl as it will cause the toffee to crystallise). Allow to set at room temperature, then break into 24 shards.

gold-lustre white chocolate lattices

white chocolate, melted

piping bag

round tip #3

greaseproof paper

gold lustre dust

On a piece of greaseproof paper, pipe the melted chocolate in a lattice pattern 4 cm long and 2.5 cm wide. Make 26 lattices. Leave the chocolate to set for 30 minutes at room temperature, or 10 minutes in the refrigerator.

Once set, use a small brush to paint each lattice with gold lustre dust.

suppliers

Barbara Jean's Cake Decorating Supplies
  Star Bowl Arcade,
  116 Fryers Street
  SHEPPARTON 3630
  phone (03) 5831 8600
Cake decorating supplies: equipment, stands,
decorations and ingredients.
Hard to find products: lustre dust, marzipan.

Cake Deco
  Shop 7, Port Phillip Arcade,
  232 Flinders Street
  MELBOURNE 3000
  phone (03) 9654 5335
  fax (03) 9654 5818
  www.cakedeco.com.au
Cake decorating supplies: equipment, stands,
decorations and ingredients.
Hard to find products: edible glitter, lustre dust,
marzipan, Wilton's food colouring.

Choice Cake Decorating Centre
  89A Switchback Road
  CHIRNSIDE PARK 3116
  phone (03) 9735 5375
  fax (03) 9735 5365
  www.choicecakes.com.au
Cake decorating supplies: equipment, stands,
decorations and ingredients.
Hard to find products: chocolate colouring,
lustre dust, marzipan, Wilton's food colouring.

Crabapple Cupcake Bakery
  Factory 37, 756 Burwood Highway
  FERNTREE GULLY 3156
  phone (03) 9752 2000
  fax (03) 9752 3777
  www.crabapplecupcakebakery.com.au

Cake decorating supplies: some decorations
and ingredients.
Hard to find products: fairies, nonpareils in
individual colours, specialty sugar flowers.

The Essential Ingredient
  Prahran Market, Elizabeth Street
  SOUTH YARRA 3141
  phone (03) 9827 9047
  fax (03) 9520 3297
  www.theessentialingredient.com.au
Cake decorating supplies: some equipment
(tins), stands, some decorations (e.g. cachous,
gold and silver leaf), and some ingredients.
Hard to find products: chocolate colouring,
marzipan, molasses and muscovado sugars.
(Note: not all products available in every store.)

Hotel Agencies
  298 Nicholson Street
  FITZROY 3065
  phone (03) 9411 8888
  fax (03) 9411 8847
  www.hotelagencies.com.au
Kitchenware and cake baking supplies:
equipment, cake stands, and electrical
appliances.

Icing On The Cake
  Shop 3, Corner of High and Sladen Streets
  CRANBOURNE 3977
  phone (03) 5996 7266
Cake decorating supplies: equipment, stands,
decorations and ingredients.
Hard to find products: edible glitter, lustre dust,
marzipan, Wilton's food colouring.

Marg & Maree's
54 Bell Street
HEIDELBERG HEIGHTS 3081
phone (03) 9455 1611
fax (03) 9455 0744
Cake decorating supplies: equipment, stands,
decorations and ingredients.
Hard to find products: chocolate colouring,
edible glitter, lustre dust, marzipan.

West's Cake Decorations
15 Florence Street
BURWOOD 3125
phone (03) 9808 3999
fax (03) 9808 5767
www.cakedecoration.com.au
West's is our supplier of choice.
Cake decorating supplies: equipment, stands,
decorations and ingredients.
Hard to find products: edible glitter, lustre dust,
Wilton's food colouring.

NEW SOUTH WALES

Bakery Sugar Craft
198 Newton Road
WETHERILL PARK 2164
phone (02) 9756 6164
fax (02) 9756 6165
www.bakerysugarcraft.com.au
Cake decorating supplies: equipment, stands,
decorations and ingredients.
Hard to find products: chocolate colouring,
edible glitter, lustre dust, Wilton's colouring.

Cupid's
Unit 2/90 Belford Street
BROADMEADOW 2292
phone (02) 4962 1884
fax (02) 4961 6594
www.cupids.idl.com.au

Cake decorating supplies: equipment, stands,
decorations and ingredients.
Hard to find products: chocolate colouring,
edible glitter, lustre dust, marzipan.

The Essential Ingredient
www.theessentialingredient.com.au

Newcastle
Shops 4–6, The Junction Fair, 200 Union Street
THE JUNCTION 2291
phone (02) 4962 3411
fax (02) 4962 3922

Sydney
477 Pacific Highway
CROWS NEST 2065
phone (02) 9439 9881
fax (02) 8905 0678

Tamworth
15 White street
TAMWORTH 2340
phone (02) 6766 5611
fax (02) 67665367

Albury
473A Dean Street
ALBURY 2640
phone (02) 6041 4111
fax (02) 6041 4112

Orange
205 Summer Street
ORANGE 2800
phone (02) 6361 8999
fax (02) 6361 7950

Cake decorating supplies: some equipment
(tins), stands, some decorations (e.g. cachous,
gold and silver leaf), and ingredients.
Hard to find products: chocolate colouring,
marzipan, molasses and muscovado sugars.

Iced Affair
  53 Church Street (Parramatta Road end)
  CAMPERDOWN 2050
  phone (02) 9519 3679
  www.icedaffair.com.au
Cake decorating supplies: equipment, stands,
decorations and ingredients.
Hard to find products: chocolate colouring,
edible glitter, lustre dust.

AUSTRALIAN CAPITAL TERRITORY

The Style Emporium
  Ginnindera Village, Gold Creek,
  O'Hanlon Place
  NICHOLLS 2913
  phone (02) 6242 5223
Cake decorating supplies: equipment, stands,
decorations and ingredients.
Hard to find products: edible glitter, lustre dust,
Wilton's food colouring.

The Essential Ingredient
  www.theessentialingredient.com.au
  52 Giles street
  KINGSTON 2604
  phone (02) 6295 7148
  fax (02) 6295 7146
Cake decorating supplies: some equipment
(tins), stands, some decorations (e.g. cachous,
gold and silver leaf), and ingredients.
Hard to find products: chocolate colouring,
marzipan, molasses and muscovado sugars.
(Note: not all products available in every store.)

SOUTH AUSTRALIA

All About Parties
  78 Tapleys Hill Road
  ROYAL PARK 5014
  phone (08) 8347 2789
Cake decorating supplies: equipment, stands,
decorations and ingredients.
Hard to find products: chocolate colouring,
edible glitter, lustre dust, Wilton's food
colouring.

Australian Cake Decoration Supplies
  240 Magill Road
  BEULAH PARK 5067
  phone (08) 8331 9399
Cake decorating supplies: equipment, stands,
decorations and ingredients.
Hard to find products: chocolate colouring,
marzipan, Wilton's food colouring.

Cake Decorator's World
  15 Newark Court
  GREENWITH 5125
  phone (08) 8396 7272
Cake decorating supplies: equipment, stands,
decorations and ingredients.
Hard to find products: edible glitter.

Cakes etc.
  305C Payneham Road,
  ROYSTON PARK 5070
  phone (08) 8362 7979
  fax (08) 8362 7979
  www.cakesetc.com.au
Cake decorating supplies: equipment, stands,
decorations, and ingredients.
Hard to find products: chocolate colouring,
edible glitter, lustre dust, Wilton's food
colouring.

Caroline's Sugar Art Services
  Shop 4, 29C Dwyer Road
  OAKLANDS PARK 5046
  phone (08) 8377 0340
  fax (08) 8377 0341
  www.carolines.com.au

Cake decorating supplies: equipment, stands, decorations, and ingredients.
Hard to find products: lustre dust, Wilton's food colouring.

Complete Cake Decorating Supplies
   Unit 1, 28 Eliza Place
   PANORAMA 5041
   phone (08) 8299 0333
Cake decorating supplies: equipment, stands, decorations, and ingredients.
Hard to find products: chocolate colouring, edible glitter, lustre dust, Wilton's food colouring.

QUEENSLAND
BB's Party Supplies & Cake Decoration
   Shop 2/481 Gympie Road
   STRATHPINE 4500
   phone (07) 3889 7547
Cake decorating supplies: decorations, and some ingredients

Cake Ornament Co.
www.cakeornament.com.au

   Head Office
   9 Counihan Road
   SEVENTEEN MILE ROCKS 4073
   phone (07) 3376 5788

   Shop 7 Wilmah Street
   ASPLEY 4034
   phone (07) 3862 9542

   Corner Kingston Road and Randall Street
   SLACKS CREEK 4127
   phone (07) 3290 0211

   Shop 4, 51 Old Cleveland Road
   CAPALABA 4157
   phone (07) 3390 1588

Cake decorating supplies: equipment, stands, decorations, and ingredients.
Hard to find products: chocolate colouring, edible glitter, lustre dust, marzipan.

Make It and Bake It
   Shop 7, Margate Shopping Centre
   266 Oxley Avenue
   MARGATE 4019
   phone (07) 3883 3444
   fax (07) 3262 8482
   www.makeitandbakeit.com.au
Cake decorating supplies: equipment, decorations, and ingredients.

WESTERN AUSTRALIA
Cake Tinz 'N' Thingz
   Unit 2/6 Corbusier Place
   BALCATTA 6021
   phone/fax (08) 9345 1869
Cake decorating supplies: equipment, stands, decorations, and ingredients.
Hard to find products: chocolate colouring, edible glitter, lustre dust, marzipan, Wilton's food colouring.

Classic Cake Decorating Supplies
   Shop16, Morley Market Shopping Centre,
   238 Walter Road
   MORLEY 6062
   phone/fax (08) 9275 7814
Cake decorating supplies: equipment, decorations, and ingredients.
Hard to find products: chocolate colouring, lustre dust, marzipan.

Major Cake Decoration Supplies
  Shop 2, 900 Albany Highway
  EAST VICTORIA PARK 6101
  phone (08) 9362 5202
  fax (08) 9355 2389
Cake decorating supplies: equipment, stands, decorations, and ingredients.
Hard to find products: chocolate colouring, edible glitter, lustre dust, Wilton's food colouring.

My Delicious Cake Decorating & Supplies
  Shop 4, 3 Lafayette Boulevard
  BIBRA LAKE 6163
  phone (08) 9418 5929
Cake decorating supplies: equipment, stands, decorations, and ingredients.
Hard to find products: chocolate colouring, lustre dust, marzipan.

Petersen's Cake Decorators Shop
  Shop 8, 370 South Street (corner Stockdale)
  O'CONNOR 6163
  phone (08) 9337 9636
  fax (08) 9331 5593
  www.cakedecoratorshop.com.au
Cake decorating supplies: equipment, stands, decorations, and ingredients.
Hard to find products: chocolate colouring, lustre dust, Wilton's food colouring.

Rawjac Enterprises
  Shop 43 Stephens Street
  BUNBURY 6230
  phone (08) 9724 1553
  fax (08) 9721 2809
  email rawjac@hotmail.com
Cake decorating supplies: equipment, stands, decorations, and ingredients.

Hard to find products: chocolate colouring, edible glitter, lustre dust, marzipan, Wilton's food colouring.

TASMANIA
Birchalls
  The Mall
  LAUNCESTON 7250
  phone (03) 6331 3011
Cake decorating supplies: equipment, stands, decorations, and ingredients.
Hard to find products: chocolate colouring, edible glitter, lustre dust.

Coryule Cake Decorating and
Chocolate Making Supplies
  Shop 7a, Bellerive Quay
  BELLERIVE 7018
  phone (03) 6244 1652
Cake decorating supplies: equipment, stands, decorations, and ingredients.
Hard to find products: chocolate colouring, edible glitter, lustre dust, marzipan, Wilton's food colouring.

acknowledgements

My greatest thanks would have to be to my husband John Graham, who gave up his secure job to support my belief in the business, and our three daughters Natalie (mum to grandson Jamie, who spent the first year of his life in a bouncinet under the kitchen table), Hayley (who created The Crabapple signature swirl) and Laura (who is still looking for a real job) for putting doubt and plans aside to get The Crabapple Cupcake Bakery to where it is today. There were times when they would start work at 8 a.m. in the morning and still be frosting cupcakes at 2 a.m. the following morning so that we had enough to take to market at 4 a.m. They are all still currently working in the business.

Thanks also to our wonderful staff: Lindy Cunningham (baker extraordinaire); Hannah Yeats (our first real employee, who helped and supported me through some of the most exhausting periods in the early days at our Tecoma shop when I was doing all the baking myself); Perri Martin (a pint-sized girl with a very big talent in cake decorating and organisation); and Sarah Matthews (who whilst studying fulltime to become a nurse would still be available and full of smiles for the early starts at the markets). Sarah has recently left us to work fulltime in nursing and we wish her the very best for the future.

A special mention to my Mum Mary Lehr (who would come in on Saturday mornings after working night shift in a hospital and spend the next 8 hours washing dishes and cleaning the shop until it shone like a new pin), and Dad Gavin Lehr (who would ring me every morning at 5 a.m. to say good morning so that I would not feel as though I was the only person up at that time of the day). Special mention has to go to my dear friend Olivia Anderson (who along with John suggested that I bake cookies and cupcakes to display on the cake stands I was selling at the markets). Olivia would always ring at just the right time to either pick me up from my negative energy, tell me off for working too hard and to not whinge to her or to give me just the advice I was looking for. Thanks also to my supportive accountant Alan Colling, CPA, who has left the business of baking and decorating to me, but has invested many personal hours in helping me organise my administrative disability.

The loyalty of our customers must not go unmentioned. Some of our customers have been following us around the markets since we started and they are the people to thank for shaping our business, as their comments and suggestions were very valuable when coming up with the flavours and designs that we produce today.

There are so many other people and institutions that have supported us throughout the last few years, including the *Age* Epicure, who have written some fabulous articles on our bakery in the past, and Adam Lancaster from OzCup/Confeta who has taken an interest in our business and directed some fabulous photography and stories to business magazines on our behalf.

I would like to thank the staff from Penguin who had to move some last minute appointments around and make new arrangements for me so that I could be given time to finish the manuscript, and work at the bakery as well.

index

the Crabapple Cupcake Bakery

FACTORY
Factory 37, 756 Burwood Highway
FERNTREE GULLY 3156
Victoria
Australia
phone (03) 9752 2000
fax (03) 9752 3777

RETAIL OUTLET
Shop 6, Prahran Market
163 Commercial Road
SOUTH YARRA 3141
Victoria
Australia
phone (03) 9827 8116
fax (03) 9827 8117

www.crabapplecupcakebakery.com.au